AFRICANS IN CHINA: GUANGDONG AND BEYOND

AFRICANS IN CHINA: GUANGDONG AND BEYOND

EDITED BY ADAMS BODOMO

DIASPORIC AFRICA PRESS

Diasporic Africa Press
New York

This book is a publication of
Diasporic Africa Press
NEW YORK | www.dafricapress.com

Copyright ©Diasporic Africa Press 2016

Library of Congress Control Number: 2016933761

ISBN-13 978-1-937306-40-3 (pbk.: alk paper)

CONTENTS

ACKNOWLEDGMENTS

We are grateful to the publisher of this edited book, Dr. Kwasi Konadu, founder of the Diasporic Africa Press, for encouraging us to put this edited volume together. The book came out of a special issue of the *Journal of Pan African Studies*, and I am grateful to its editor, Dr. Itibari Zulu, for permission to republish revised and updated versions of the papers. I thank each of the authors for their hard work and for responding to critiques for the betterment of the book. Finally yet importantly, I thank my editorial assistants Caroline Pajancic and Dr. Che Dewei for several rounds of proofreading and formatting that helped produce this important volume on the African diaspora in China.

INTRODUCTION

AFRICANS IN CHINA: ISSUES AND REVIEWS

ADAMS BODOMO

The chapters of this book were first published as articles in a special issue of the *Journal of Pan African Studies* dedicated to research on the African diaspora in China. They have been subsequently revised and updated for this edited volume. Africa-China relations have increasingly constituted a prominent research topic in many humanities and social sciences disciplines since 2000. An important aspect of this research theme is dedicated to issues of migration between Africa and China and the formation of diaspora communities in these two parts of the world. We often hear of research on Africans in China and Chinese in Africa. There is, however, a tendency to conflate the two quite distinct phenomena into "Chinese in Africa/ Africans in China," though these are disparate migratory and diaspora phenomena.

This book is dedicated solely to exploring the African presence in China and the formation of African diaspora communities in Guangzhou, Yiwu, Shanghai, Beijing, Hong Kong, Macau, and many other prominent locations within Greater China. There is already a significant body of research that answer empirical questions such as why Africans go to China, the major cities in which Africans visit and live, what they do there, and how they are received by the Chinese state and the Chinese people. In this introduction to the volume, I first review the issues involved in the rise of a new African diaspora in China, and then outline the various places in China where the African presence is most prominent. Finally, I introduce the chapters featured in the book.

ISSUES

With China's entry into the World Trade Organization in December 2001, there was a dramatic increase in the number of Africans coming to China to buy goods for sale back in Africa. This has created a visible presence of Africans in Guangzhou, which has been receiving, in many cases, a lot of negative coverage in newspapers and magazines on issues of immigration irregularities. However, behind all these negative newspapers reports, there are many positive stories about the presence and impact of Africans in China. In particular, their substantial contributions to the development of Africa-China relations are rarely recognized. It has been necessary to do in-depth, on-site studies beyond the occasional one-day journalistic or fly-by academic coverage in order to understand the African presence in China better. Despite the negative news coming out of Guangzhou, there are a substantial number of Africans who are employed and engaged in both the formal and informal economies of China in other major cities such as Hong Kong, Macau, Yiwu, Shanghai, and, of course, Beijing. What are these Africans doing in China? How are they received? And how does their presence contribute to an understanding of larger issues about Africa-in-China and China-in-Africa?

Contributors to this book thematically address the African presence in China through the lens of history, society, culture, language, and Africa-China relations. Specifically, they engage the following questions: How do these Africans influence their Chinese hosts and how do the Chinese influence the Africans? How does the African presence in China affect trade between Africa and China and how do these Africans contribute to the economies of the countries from which they originate? Is this new and emerging African diaspora in China different from other African diasporas? What theoretical and methodological insights does the study of these African migrants in China have on migration and diaspora studies?

SNAPSHOTS FROM MAJOR CHINESE CITIES

In this part of the introduction, I outline the main parts and cities in China where the African presence is more prominent. These include six main places: Guangzhou, Yiwu, Shanghai, Beijing, Hong Kong, and Macau. I emphasize areas that have received the least coverage, in this volume and elsewhere, so readers will have the widest context for understanding the evolving African presence in China.

Guangzhou is the capital of Guangdong, the richest and most industrial province in China. Guangzhou boasts the largest population of Africans in China, and thus this concentration of Africans in China has received the most attention from researchers. The work of four leading groups of researchers stand out among the rest: Li Zhigang and his collaborators (e.g. Li et al 2009), Bodomo and his collaborators (e.g. Bodomo, 2012, 2010, Bodomo and Ma, 2010, 2012), Joseph Tucker and his collaborators (e.g. Hall et al 2014), and Haugen (2012, 2013). Other works include Bertoncello and Bredeloup (2007), Bredeloup (2012), Han (2013), Le Bail (2009), Mueller and Wehrhahn (2013), Castillo (2014), and Lan (2014). Most of the contributions in this volume describe aspects of Africans in Guangzhou. There are approximately 100,000 Africans in Guangzhou, but substantial numbers are being registered in neighboring cities like Shenzhen, Dongguan and Foshan (e.g. Bork et al, 2014).

Yiwu, in Zhejiang Province, is home to currently the fastest growing African population, currently estimated at about 30,000 (Bodomo and Ma, 2010). Unlike Guangzhou, where there are more Africans from "Sub-Saharan" Africa, in Yiwu we have more individuals from the northwest region of Africa and increasingly from the Horn of Africa. Both groups of Africans are established traders and also have businesses that cater to the large number of visitors from Africa and other places that come to buy goods at China's largest commodities market, which is located in Yiwu (Bodomo and Ma, 2012, 2012; Le Bail, 2009; Cissé, 2013). However, very little has been written on the second largest set of African communities in Yiwu. Yiwu is one area scholars need to pay greater attention, beyond the apparent over-concentration on Africans in Guangzhou. Fortunately, this book has two chapters that cover important aspects of African life in Yiwu.

Shanghai is often tooted as the largest, most sophisticated, and most cosmopolitan city in China, but when one looks at this city from the perspective of the African presence in China, this perception of Shanghai is highly debatable. Shanghai does not have a Chung King Mansions like Hong Kong, a San Ma Lou like Macau, nor a Tianxiu Mansions like Guangzhou. Indeed, rather than speak of the African presence in Shanghai, Bodomo (2012) reminds us of the African absence in Shanghai. With the exception of online communities of Africans in Shanghai, there are hardly any public places where one can observe Africans congregating in Shanghai, contrary to what happens in Hong Kong, Macau, Guangzhou, and Yiwu. It is not that there are no Africans or Black people in Shanghai—I estimate some 3,000 Africans who communicate mostly online in Shanghai—it is just that they are rare, comprising mostly students who are normally found on university campuses. Of course, the situation can change rapidly anytime, especially with the establishment of many African consulates in the city, which is likely to attract many African businesses catering to the African diplomatic community there.

Beijing is the capital of China and home to the most diversified African community. There are more Africans on official duty for their countries and international institutions in Beijing. We have ambassadors, consuls, and other diplomats; bankers and accountants for financial institutions; and students in the most prominent universities and colleges in Beijing. African community members, unlike in Shanghai, are very visible at major public spaces such as Sanlitun—world famous for its street bars and international stores. There are also well-established and quite famous African restaurants like the erstwhile Pilipili and Toure House, where various kinds of networks have developed. Altogether, I estimate the number of Africans in Beijing to be about 50,000. As China's most international city, Hong Kong has a sizeable population of foreign residents, some of whom have become permanent residents or taken up Hong Kong citizenship. The most prominent publications specifically devoted to Africans in Hong Kong include those by Bodomo (2007, 2009, and 2012), Mathews and Yang (2012), and Wong and Tang's chapter in this volume.

Among the permanent residents are some 2,000 Africans, particularly White South Africans, but also a substantial number from West and East African countries. It is very difficult to get reliable figures about Africans in Hong Kong because authorities would often not obtain or keep statistics for Africa and a few other regions, for which they reserve a category called "Others." Nevertheless, a substantial number of non-permanent residents are now in the city as traders, artists, tourists, along with a few who claim to be refugees seeking asylum. Altogether, I would put the number of Africans in Hong Kong at 20,000. These Africans in Hong Kong have developed networks and even communities over the years, members of which constantly interact with each other. The best place to observe the African presence in Hong Kong is at the world-famous Chung King Mansions on Nathan Road in the Tsim Sha Tsui district of Kowloon, where they can be observed buying and selling goods such as mobile phones and fabrics. Even though the Chung King Mansions have served as the most prominent space to showcase the African population (Bodomo, 2007), the African community in Hong Kong is far more than Chung King Mansions. These networks have branched out and many African communities and networks have coalesced or taken shape around African businesses such as restaurants and hair salons.

Macau, like Hong Kong, is an international city with substantial numbers of foreigners, especially from Lusophone countries such as Portugal (which colonized Macau until 1999), Brazil, Angola, Mozambique, Guinea Bissau, and Cape Verde. There are currently three major published studies on Africans in Macau: Morais (2009), Bodomo (2012), and Bodomo & Silva (2012). Macau has the most established and most organized African community in China. Its members, predominantly from the Lusophone countries of Africa, are tightly connected by the Portuguese language. Many of them are within the civil service as administrators, lawyers, accountants, and other professionals. However, there is an increasing presence of other Africans, without established professions, that hang around the San Ma Lou shopping mall—a relative equivalent of the Chung King Mansions in Hong Kong. Altogether, I estimate the number of Africans in Macau to be around 10,000. Beyond the major six cities, African communities are beginning to be noticed in other major cities in Greater China such as most provincial capitals, especially those in the southern parts of the country including Nanjing, Chengdu, Chongqing, and Nanning, and of course in Taiwanese cities such as Taipei, where a lot of research remains to be done.

CHAPTERS IN THE BOOK

While building on the works mentioned above, the six main chapters in this volume address theoretical and methodological issues as well. Many of the authors have developed theoretical formulations to explain the African presence in China, addressing the four main competing theories or metaphors that have emerged: the migrant community as an enclave, the migrant community as an outpost, the migrant community as a bridge between source and host communities, and the migrant community as a networked community. More importantly, they have proposed new theoretical frameworks based on thorough overviews of the African presence in China.

In chapter 1, Li Anshan of Peking University, one of the most senior African specialists in China, provides one of the best historical overview of the African diaspora in China. It is a reflection on the exciting historical links between Africa and China. The presence of Africans in China dates to the Tang Dynasty (618-907 CE). The author anchors the links between Africa and China in the historical record, and then explores the challenges and opportunities of the African diaspora in contemporary China. The second chapter by Daouda Cissé is one of the few studies on African traders in Yiwu, based on detailed observations in the field and on discussions with African and Chinese traders using the Bamana(kan), Chinese, English, and Wolof languages. Empirically rich, the chapter makes an important contribution through its focus on African traders in Yiwu and their trade networks as well as their role in the distribution of Chinese consumer goods in African markets.

The third chapter by Laurence Marfaing and Alena Thiel will certainly increase our knowledge about network theory concerning the African diaspora in China. With a sound empirical basis, their discussion of the relationships between "networks of accumulation" and "networks of survival" about Africans in China will likely be a key topic of discussion among scholars of the African diaspora in Asia. Like the previous chapter on Yiwu, this chapter is empirically rich, and makes an important contribution towards our understanding of African traders in Yiwu, Guangzhou and Hong Kong and the networks they have developed between Africa and China. In Chapter 4, Carlton Jama Adams's study principally uses interviews of people of African descent in Guangzhou and Shanghai to offer an exciting perspective for understanding issues in diaspora studies using the notion of "adaptive ambivalence." This notion aptly captures the often-ambivalent responses of "Africana" immigrants in China—by "Africana," we mean peoples from Africa and the worldwide African diaspora. For those interviewed, they may love their countries of origins yet find that they have to emigrate; they complain about their host country, yet still perceive more opportunities there than in their home countries. According to Adams, "Many contemporary immigrants adopt a stance of adaptive ambivalence with regards to both home and host country. They find admirable and constraining qualities in both cultures. As a rule, Africana immigrants closely identify with the aesthetics (food, weather, vistas) and relationships of their homeland while bemoaning its structural limitations as manifested in the lack of opportunities for intellectual growth and access to material goods. By way of contrast, China is admired for the availability of resources to develop intellectually and to acquire wealth. At the same time its questionable ethics, its polluted environment and its ambivalence toward foreigners is a source of stress."

Co-authored by Gordon Chak-pong Tsui and Hayes Hei-hang Tang, chapter 5 explores the motivations as well as aspirations that make people from Africa want to study in Hong Kong. Using in-depth data collected from 10 students, the authors gather that the high quality of education as well as adequate financial aid offered by the University of Hong Kong are the two leading motivating factors for students choosing the university over several others in the world. If universities are seeking ways to attract international students, this chapter would be a valuable source of information. In the sixth and final chapter, Adams Bodomo and Caroline Pajancic address a major challenge faced by most researchers: getting an estimate, in the absence of accurate official figures, for the number of Africans presently in Greater China. The authors indicate there are between 400,000 and 500,000 Africans in China during any given year. Of that estimated total, there are at least 300,000 to 400,000 traders, 30,000 to 40,000 students, 4,000 to 5000 professionals, 10,000 to 100,000 tourists and 10,000 to 20,000 temporary business travelers. The chapter argues for a mixture of qualitative and quantitative methods in further research of this nature.

This introduction has outlined some central issues concerning the African diaspora of some half a million members in China and provided a simplified overview of Africans in various parts of China. The African diaspora in China is in its early stages of establishment, and is thus constantly evolving. The six chapters in this volume are among the first to draw attention to this novelty and, taken together, act as compasses to guide scholars and other observers of this important process of globalization in the twenty-first century.

REFERENCES

Bertoncello, B. and Sylvie Bredeloup (2007) The emergence of new African "Trading posts" in Hong Kong and Guangzhou. *China Perspectives*, No.1, pp 94 -105.

Bodomo, A. (2007) An Emerging African-Chinese Community in Hong Kong: The Case of Tsim Sha Tsui's Chungking Mansions, In Kwesi Kwaa Prah (ed). *Afro-Chinese Relations: Past, Present and Future. Cape Town, South Africa.* The Center for Advanced Studies in African Societies, 367-389.

Bodomo, A. (2009) Africa-China relations: symmetry, soft power, and South Africa. *The China Review: An Interdisciplinary Journal on Greater China*, Vol. 9, No. 2 (Fall 2009), 169-178.

Bodomo, A. (2010) The African trading community in Guangzhou: an emerging bridge for Africa-China relations. *China Quarterly. Volume 203, 693 – 707.*

Bodomo, A. (2012) *Africans in China: A Sociocultural Study and Its Implications for Africa-China Relations.* Amherst, New York: Cambria Press.

Bodomo, A. and Grace Ma. (2010) From Guangzhou to Yiwu: Emerging facets of the African diaspora in China. *International Journal of African Renaissance Studies* 5(2), 283-289.

Bodomo, A. and Grace Ma. (2012) We are what we eat: food in the process of community formation and identity shaping among African traders in Guangzhou and Yiwu. *African Diaspora* 5(1), 1-26.

Bodomo, A. and Roberval Silva. (2012) Language matters: the role of linguistic identity in the establishment of the lusophone African community in Macau. *African Studies* 71(1), 71-90.

Bork-Hüffer, Etzold, Gransow, Tomba, Sterly, Suda, Kraas & Flock (2014): Agency and the Making of Transient Urban Spaces: Examples of Migrants in the City in the Pearl River Delta, China and Dhaka, Bangladesh. In: Population, Space and Place (online first). DOI: 10.1002/psp.1890. *http://onlinelibrary.wiley.com/doi/10.1002/psp.1890/abstract*

Bredeloup, S (2012) African trading posts in Guangzhou: emergent or recurrent commercial form? *African Diaspora* 5(1): 27 – 50

Castillo, Roberto (2014) "Feeling at home in the "Chocolate City": an exploration of place-making practices and structures of belonging amongst Africans in Guangzhou." Inter-Asia Cultural Studies 15 (2): 1-23.

Cissé, D. (2013) South-South Migration and Sino-African Small Traders: A Comparative Study of Chinese in Senegal and Africans in China. *African Review of Economics and Finance* 5(1), 17-30.

Hall, B., Chen, W., Latkin, C., Ling, L, Tucker, J. (2014) Africans in south China face social and health barriers. *The Lancet*, vol 283, Issue 9925, 1291—1292, 12th April 2014

Han, H. (2013) Individual Grassroots Multilingualism in Africa Town in Guangzhou: The Role of States in Globalization. *International Multilingual Research Journal* 7(1), 83-97.

Haugen, H. Ø. (2012) Nigerians in China: A second state of immobility. *International Migration* 50(2), 65-80.

Haugen, H. Ø. (2013) African pentecostal migrants in China: Marginalization and the alternative geography of a mission theology. *African Studies Review.* 56(1), 81-102

Lan, Shanshan. (2014) State regulation of undocumented African migrants in China: A multi-scalar analysis. *Journal of Asian and African Studies* Vol. X 1-16

Le Bail, H. (2009). Foreign Migrations to China's City-Markets: the case of African merchants. *Asie Visions* 19.

Li, Zhigang, Laurence Ma and Desheng Xue. (2009) An African enclave in China: The making of a new transnational urban space. *Eurasian Geography and Economics* 50(6), 699—719.

Mathews, G. and Yang, Y. (2012) How Africans Pursue Low-End Globalization in Hong Kong and Mainland China. *Journal of Current Chinese Affairs* 41(2).

Morais, I. (2009) "China wahala": The tribulations of Nigerian "Bushfallers" in a Chinese Territory. *Transtext(e)s Transcultures. Journal of Global Cultural Studies* 5. Retrieved 24 May 2010 from Transtext(e)s Transcultures database available from the Revues Website: http://transtexts.revues.org/index281.html

Müller, A. and Wehrhahn, R. (2013) Transnational business networks of African intermediaries in China: Practices of networking and the role of experiential knowledge. *DIE ERDE–Journal of the Geographical Society of Berlin*, 144(1), 82-97.

AFRICAN DIASPORA IN CHINA: REALITY, RESEARCH AND REFLECTION[1]

LI ANSHAN

INTRODUCTION

The history of human beings is a history of (im)migration. From the ancient times, people moved from one place to another to find better environments for survival or development. After the modern international system came into being with nation-states making borders a necessity, immigration became an issue, be it from national policy or international concerns. With the recent development of China-Africa relations, a wave of bilateral migration occurred.[2] This phenomenon created an enthusiasm for the study of migration between China and Africa. There are studies on Chinese either on the African continent (Li, 2000, 2006, 2012a), on particular regions (Ly Tio Fane-Pines, 1981, 1985), or on different countries (Human 1984; Yap & Leong, 1996; Wong-Hee-kan, 1996; Ly-Tio-Fane Pineo & Lim Fat, 2008; Park, 2008), yet the African diaspora in China is much less studied. As A. Bodomo correctly points out "Africans did not just start moving into China in the 21st century.... [T]his history must be placed in the context of the wider African presence in Asia, which itself has not yet been the subject of sustained research" (Bodomo, 2012). This chapter constitutes a historiography of the African presence in China; it is aimed at getting a clearer understanding of the connections between reality and research, and if possible, provide some indication for future study. It is divided into four parts: blacks/Africans in early China, the issue of *Kunlun*, the

origin and jobs of blacks/Africans in ancient China, and the study
of Africans in contemporary China. The term "blacks" or "black
people" are used in the chapter to indicate various black peoples in
Chinese history, including different types of people, e.g., the Negroid, Oceanic Negroid, Negrito and others.

WERE AFRICANS IN CHINA IN EARLY TIMES?

There is a long history of China-Africa contact, illustrated by Chinese classics such as dynastic histories and classics by Du Huan,
Duan Chengshi, Zhou Qufei, Zhao Rukuo, Wang Dayuan, Fei
Xin, Ma Huan, etc., and contemporary studies (Dart, 1925; Zhang,
1930, 1977 [1930]; Cen, 1935; Duyvendak, 1947; Filesi, 1972; Ma
& Meng, 1987; Shen, 1989; Brunson, 1995; Li, 2006, 2012a; Wyatt, 2010).[3] Yet whether Africans existed in early China is another
question. Scholars have done studies on blacks in China since the
nineteenth century, yet the blacks mentioned in their works seem
to be "Pygmy," "Negrito," or Oceanic "Negroids" of the Melanesian
type (Lacouperie, 1887; Li, 1928; Weidenreich, 1939; Ling, 1956;
Coon, 1963; Yang, 1995). It is also suggested that blacks in early
China were related to Rouzhi (pronounced as Yuezhi, Yueshi) or Persian (Chen, 1993; Schafer, 1991: 46).

   Chinese historians generally agree that blacks/Africans came to
China during the Tang Dynasty, 618-907 CE (Zhang, 1928, 1930;
Xu, 1984; Ai, 1987; Jing, 1998). Yet archaeological discoveries challenge this view. Archeological evidence indicates the possibility of
contact between China and Africa in an earlier time. An excavation
report on the Shang Dynasty (seventeenth to eleventh century BCE)
sites at Anyang, the capital of Shang, shows that there are similarities
between the skull that was discovered and that of the Oceanic Negroids and black African (Chang, 1968; Yang, 1969). Many Negroid
images in stone, metal and jade were also found in Anyang. Sati bur-
ial existing in Nubia, Egypt and Mesopotamia, thousands of cowrie
shells used for money and more than five hundred of jade objects
were also discovered in the tomb of Lady Fu Hao (fourteenth century BCE), who served as the principal consort and general to Shang
King, Wu Ding, described as the "evidence of African participa-

tion in royalty" by Brunson, who concluded that "[I]t can be safely estimated that an African presence existed in China from a most remote period and an evolution of this physical type is an indigenous phenomenon" (Brunson, 1985). The estimation is rather bold. In Guangzhou, a city of south China, more than 1,000 tombs of the Han Dynasty have been excavated since the 1950s, where 152 pottery figures were found, some looking like blacks (Qin 2010). Three explanations were offered for the origin of the blacks—blacks from islands near Indochina, indigenous people of Indonesia, and people of West Asia or East Africa (Guangzhou Shi, 1981). *Qilin*, an imagined fortunate animal in ancient China, appeared in a stone sculpture in the Han Dynasty (202 BCE-220 CE), resembling a giraffe (Xuzhou Museum, 1980), as indicated in figure 1.[4]

Figure 1: Qilin in stone sculpture in the Han Dynasty (202 BCE-220 CE) resembling a giraffe.

During the Han Dynasty, Ethiopia and Alexandria were mentioned in *Shi Ji* (Records of the Grand Historian, 104-91 BCE), *Han Shu* (History of the Han, 80 CE) and *Wei Lue* (Brief Accounts on the Wei Kingdom). The astronomer-geographer Claudius Ptolemaeus of Alexandria described China and the silk-road in his *Geography* in the second century. The earliest indication of blacks (*hei-se-ren*) in China seems to be in *Juyan Han Jian*.[5] Sixty pieces of *Juyan Han Jian* recorded individuals with their identity, such as *jun* (as prefecture, unit above county), *xian* (county), *li* (grassroots unit), rank, age, height and skin color. With height and skin color as identity elements, it is possible to understand the physical features of individuals at the time. Two studies are particularly interesting. According to Zhang's study, 55 cases with skin color are identified among 60 individual cases, and 53 recorded as "black."[6] In addition, one was labeled "brown black" and another "yellow black." This is very impressive even considering that Han China was a multi-ethnic empire. Were the black-skinned people from a specific area? Or did they belong to a *zhongzu* (ethnic group or race) different from the Han Chinese? The significance of the study lies in the analysis of height and color, two of the physical characteristics of the Chinese in the Han period. The author argued that since the 53 black-skinned individuals were from different parts of the empire, they were ordinary Han Chinese and did not belong to one or more specific *zhongzu* that was different from the Han Chinese (Zhang, 1977).

Yang came to a different conclusion after the study of *Juyan Hanjian* and related literature such as *Yilin* which were published almost at the same time. First, there were hundreds of thousands of foreigners living in the Hexi area and the surrounding area of Chang-an, the capital at the time and an international metropolis. Second, most of the black-skinned people lived in the Hexi area, a fact that Zhang failed to explain. Among 25 cases of the black-skinned people in the records of *Ji-guan* (birth place or origin), 17 were from the Hexi area. Thirdly, the height of the blacks was generally 165.6-177.1cm, taller than ordinary Chinese (161.2-167.6cm) but similar to the Nilotic black in Northeast Africa or the Pamiri. Fourth, married black-skinned men positioned as border officials who lived with their families should have settled in the region much earlier, possibly at the beginning of Emperor Zhaodi's rule (94-74 BCE). Fifth, two black women in *Yilin* with sunken eyes lived a different life not married to Han Chinese. This should be regarded as different pattern of culture. Yang believes that the blacks may have been foreigners who came from overseas, most probably from the Western Region, a specific term for the Chinese to describe the vast area west of China (Yang, 1995). The conclusion is that there were blacks in early China, possibly of foreign origin, or even of African origin.

After a long period of war and instability, China entered an era of prosperity in the Tang Dynasty (618-907 CE). Foreigners came to China as diplomats, officials, visitors, traders, workers, etc., and some settled down in China. Two terms, *Sengzhi* and *Kunlun*, appeared in the literature to refer to the blacks. The record shows that in the year 724 two *Sengzhi* (Zandj) girls from the Kingdom of Palembang were offered to the Chinese Emperor, and four *Sengzhi* slaves, five *Sengzhi* boys and two *Sengzhi* girls were sent to Emperor Xian Zhong (805-820 CE) in 813, 815 and 818, respectively, all from islands of the present Indonesia as tribute. *Kunlun,* used as a name for mountain, water or place (Goodrich, 1931), official position and state, in ancient time, turned out to be a name for an ethnic group with a specific meaning, e.g., the blacks (Zhang, 1930; Ge, 2001).

KUNLUN OR BLACK PEOPLE: DIFFERENT VIEWS
AND ETHNOCENTRISM

There was an increase in the number of blacks during the Tang and Song dynasties (960-1279, CE) and *Kunlun* became a fashionable topic (more than *Sengzhi*) in the literature.[7] Who were the *Kunlun* people? Where did they come from? What did they do in ancient China? There are three kinds of evidence supporting the presence of *Kunlun* during that period—paintings, pottery figures, and literature.

Dunhuang is located in Northwest China, where there are hundreds of Buddhist caves in which the paintings of the Tang Dynasty are preserved. Among the famous Dunhuang wall-paintings, quite a few of them contain black-skinned figures, such as Dunhuang Yulin Cave No. 23, Dunhuang Caves No. 103, 194, 220, 332, 335, 431, etc. Black people also appeared in paintings as well. Secondly, from the 1940s on, many black pottery figures were discovered in Xi-an (formerly Chang-an) area, the former capital of the ancient dynasties. The pottery figures aroused excitement among archeologists. One in Madam Pei's tomb (850 CE) in Xi-an is obviously a Negroid—15 cm tall, with curly hair, red lips, white eyes, high and wide

nose, impressive muscles and short in body, a typical African figure
(Du, 1979), as shown in figure 2.

*Figure 2: Black pottery figure in Madam Pei's tomb (850 CE)
found in 1954 in Xi-an.*

Thirdly, *Kunlun* or blacks became a rather popular subject in various
writings during the Tang Dynasty and beyond, either in official
works or in literature, such as *Jiu Tang Shu, Xin Tang Shu, Zizhi
Tongjian, Tang Hui Yao, Cefu Yuangui, Youyang Zazu, Taiping
Guangji, Zhu Fan Zhi, Pingzhou Ketan,* etc. Therefore, there are
quite a few studies on the topic by contemporary scholars, either
during the Tang period, or the dynasties afterwards (Zhang, 1930,
1977; Duyvendak, 1947; Filesi, 1972; Du, 1979; Xu, 1980, 1983,
1984; Brunson, 1985; Ai, 1987; Jing, 1998; Ge, 2001; Wilensky,
2002; Smidt, 2009; Wyatt, 2010).

Regarding the identity of *Kunlun*, there are generally two views: they are either seen as Negroid from Africa or as Negrito from Southeast Asia. Zhang Xinglang (originally spelt Chang Hsing-lang), who made a great contribution to the study of China-foreign relations, published in 1930 an article in English and a collection of rich materials of *Kunlun* in the Tang literature. The article dealt with eight issues, trying to identify *Kunlun*, their origin and the linkage with the Arabs, and instances of the use of the terms *Kunlun* and *Kunlun nu* (*Kunlun* slave) in Chinese literature. Zhang's conclusions are very affirmative. The land of *Kunlun* is present Siam, which had nothing to do with *Kunlun* as people. *Kunlun* or *Kunlun nu* was used frequently to describe black servants or slaves in China; they were from *Kunlun Cengqi* which was identical to Zanzibar (Zhao, 1225) and usually brought to China by Arabs who were involved in trafficking slaves for a long time, some imported through the South Sea. His conclusion is that the *Kunlun nu* were not from Zhenla (present Cambodia) or Southeast Asia, a view put forward by scholars in the Qing Dynasty (1616-1911); they were black slaves from Africa (Zhang, 1930, 1977 [1930]). His works provided a convenient access to the international academia (Goodrich, 1931), yet his problem is also obvious. By using subtitles such as "The verification of *Kunlun nu*," "The origin of *Kunlun nu*" or "The trade of *Kunlun nu* to China," together with his argument, the specious generalization that all the *Kunlun* were slaves is far from the truth, which has greatly influenced the latter study at home and abroad.

Zhang is supported by many scholars (Hu & Zhang, 1961; Zhang, 1963; Xu, 1983; Zhang, 1987; Jing, 1998). They argued that China-Africa relations started very early, and quoted Zhang's view directly or indirectly, indicating the blacks were from Africa. How did Africans come to China during the Tang Dynasty? Since a sea route between Dar Es Salaam and China was recorded in *Xin Tangshu* (History of New Tang, 1060 CE), some scholars suggest that the Africans came through the sea, or "Silk Road" by sea (Shen, 1985, 1990; Jing, 1998). Ai argued that before the sixteenth century, blacks were mostly sent, not sold, by Persians, Arabs or Javanese to Chinese authorities. There was no road from Africa to China for slaves to be transported. After the Atlantic slave trade started, Europeans brought Africans to China, the Dutch had black slaves in Taiwan, the Portuguese took them to Macao, the British and French used them as servants in coastal China. During the Ming and Qing Dynasties, the Chinese government prohibited the entrance of black slaves into China and the capture or use of Chinese as slaves by colonialists (Ai, 1987).

In 2001, Chinese historian Ge Chengyong criticized Zhang's view in an article that probed the origin of the blacks living in Chang-an city in the Tang Dynasty and drew a conclusion different from Zhang's. Considering the "African origin" thesis unconvincing, he suggested that the blacks were not Negroid from Africa but Negrito from Nan Hai (south sea, present Southeast Asia). Some of the *Kunlun* were part of foreigners' annual tribute to Chinese authorities, some were left in China by foreign envoys, and some were slaves sold to the coastal regions. As for the term *Sengzhi*, it is generally considered to be identical to Zanj (e.g., Zinj, Zenj, Zandj, Zanghi) and is a word used by the Arabs to refer to the East African coast. "It still survives in the name Zanzibar. The Arabs called the Africans who came from the East African coast, the Zanji" (Rashidi, 2010: 143). Ge disagreed with the view, suggesting *Sengzhi* was an expression of Buddhism in Nanhai in early times. For Ge, it is more proper to look for the origins of the blacks in Southeast Asia rather than in Africa (Ge, 2001), a view that is accepted by scholars in China (e.g. Cheng, 2002; Liang, 2004).

There are few studies on blacks in pre-modern China in international academia for a couple of reasons, and the mastery of classical Chinese is apparently an important one. The works by Julie Wilensky and Don Wyatt are exceptional. Wilensky's article made a detailed study on the concept of *Kunlun* and the shifts in Chinese perceptions of people with dark skin and Chinese knowledge of Africa in ancient China. Although the author borrowed heavily on Zhang's work in the first two chapters, her mastery of Chinese is impressive. The work used various Chinese sources of dynastic histories, fictional literature, geographical and travel notes, etc. The writings of officials are important sources in the article, such as Customs official Zhao Rukuo, or Fei Xin and Ma Huan who both worked in Zheng He's fleet as a navy official and interpreter, respectively. Owing to the long period and the enormous materials on the subject, the conclusion is somewhat ambiguous. On the one hand, the author acknowledged that "[i]t is difficult to assess the complex legacy of pre-modern Chinese perceptions of Africa and dark-skinned people." On the other hand, it is concluded that the Chinese have had specific "negative attitudes towards Africans and other people with dark skin" (Wilensky, 2002: 43), which is a rather common view (Dikotter, 1992; Wyatt, 2010).

Wyatt's book is also an important work in the field, although less promising as the ambitious title suggests. As professor of history, Wyatt is skillful enough to make maximum use of two pieces of information. One is a paragraph recorded in the dynastic history of Tang of the murder of Lu Yuanrui, the rapacious governor who wanted to cheat foreign merchants in the sale of their goods. Accidentally, the murderer was a courageous *Kunlun*, who not only killed the governor in front of his guards, but also other officials, and successfully escaped. The author put the case in a broad historical context and elaborated on the implications of the murder by a Kunlun. Another is Zhu Yu's *Pingzhou Ketan* (Tales of Pingzhou, 1119 CE), a collection of anecdotal trifles and notes which described the social life of Guangzhou, especially that of foreign residents. It contains several references to *Kunlun* as domestic slaves, and laborers employed on a shipboard to caulk leaky seams below the water-line from the outside as they were expert swimmers. "However, for any modern Western observer who, more than a millennium after the fact, seeks to penetrate and decipher this most unexpected of references in a premodern Chinese text, understandably and justifiably, endeavors to reconstitute the context of Zhu Yu's striking commentary depend most of all on the question of origins. In short, who were these slaves?" (Wyatt, 2010: 55). Did he find the answer? Yes, it was "nowhere else than Africa" (Wyatt, 2010: 10, 78), a conclusion made by Zhang eighty years ago.

Taiping Guangji (Comprehensive Collections of the Taiping Era, 978 CE) is a work containing various stories of *Kunlun* as positive figures.[8] It is interesting that Wyatt did not quote anything from the book except in a footnote. Why? One reason might be that the book is fictional, therefore not worthwhile as evidence. Yet fiction is a meaningful form which reflects the reality and social or ideological change, and a historian should use any material possible to explain what happened. Intentional or unintentional bias might be another reason, since the cases in the book are contrary to Wyatt's views.[9] For example, Mo Kunlun, a black boy was born in an unusual way after his mother's dream of an alien monk, yet grew up as a brave guard and lived a happy life accorded by the emperor. Another case is *Kunlun Nu*,[10] a fictional story with a strong, smart and brave *Kunlun* hero named Mole who helped his master in a unique way.[11] Do the positive figures reflect something in the period?

Since *Kunlun* or *Kunlun nu* was frequently used during the period referring to blacks and has the connotation of "race" and color, I would like to make two points. First, ethnocentrism is a universal phenomenon. Second, Chinese prejudice was against all foreigners, not just "Africans and other people with dark skin." Ethnocentrism (different from William Graham Sumner's notion) is an attitude or action of a group of people who regard themselves as normal, beautiful and clever while looking down upon other human groups, which usually involves the use of derogatory terms to describe them. Ethnocentrism is universal between any groups of people without communication and mutual understanding, especially in ancient times. As Wyatt correctly points out, "during this period in global history, so much before the time when frequent transcontinental contact would begin to become commonplace, people were willing to believe or at least entertain even the most prejudicial and outlandish things about people foreign to themselves" (Wyatt, 2010). The Romans looked at all non-Romans as barbarians and the Greeks regarded themselves the most civilized in the world. The Indians thought they were living in the center of the world (as the Chinese did). Africans had prejudices against the whites. Ibn Battuta told us that Malian cannibals, if we are to believe him, did not eat the whites, since "eating a white man is harmful because he is not ripe" (Hamdun & King, 1975: 51; Ibn Battuta, 1929). Winnie Mandela described her grandma as the first racist she ever met, because she told Winnie the whites must be sick with their blue eyes and pale skin (Mandela, 1985).

The Chinese were "by no means immune to such willfully misanthropic misconceptions" (Wyatt, 2010: 65). Being self-centered and conceited, the Chinese looked down upon others, using derogatory names to describe their neighbors in all four directions, e.g., *dong yi* (east barbarian), *nan man* (south barbarian), *xi rong* (west barbarian) and *bei di* (north barbarian). In the extreme cases, foreigners were called *gui* (devil), not human. They termed the blacks as *fan nu* (barbarian slaves), *hei gui* (black devils) or *Kunlun nu* (Kunlun slaves), and named whites *yang guizi* (foreign devils), *hong mao gui* (red-haired devil), *fangou* (barbarian dog) or *gui lao* (devil male) and *gui po* (devil female) (Dikotter, 1992).[12] Keeping this in mind, we can understand that Chinese prejudice was against not just only blacks but also whites, or any "others" for that matter. Yet if ethnocentrism changes to racism which was mobilized to justify the action of militarily suppressing, economically exploiting, and politically dominating other human groups as modern colonialism did, it is another story which goes beyond this chapter.

KUNLUN OR THE BLACKS: THEIR ORIGINS AND JOBS IN CHINA

As mentioned above, foreigners were present in China during the Han Dynasty, and during Tang and in Song China resumed an empire with many metropolitan cities hosting foreign residents. The cities enjoyed their international fame, such as Chang-an, Guangzhou, and Quanzhou. As the capital of the Han, Chang-an during the Tang Dynasty attracted again many foreigners, including prosperous Arabs, Indians and other Asians. Guangzhou in the south with a reputation for foreign traders had close relations with the outside world even during the Han period. Another southern port, Quanzhou, was named *Shijing Shizhou Ren* (city with people from ten continents) or "foreigner's port" at the time and continued to be reputed as "the most important port in the world" in the Song and Yuan (1206-1368 CE).

As early as the Dong Jin Dynasty (317-420 CE), *Kunlun* was used
to describe blacks in dynastic history, but that is no indication that
black slaves were known in China at the time, as Zhang suggested
(Zhang, 1930: 44). The term *Kunlun Ren* (Kunlun people), not *Kunlun nu*, appeared in *Sui Shu* (History of the Sui Dynasty, 636 CE)
However, Arabs carried on with trade activities on the East African
coast for a long time; black slaves were just one of many commodities (Beachey, 1976; Segal, 2001). With many Arab merchants
coming to China, they brought blacks with them as attendants,
porters, and slaves who they presented to the Chinese authorities as
gifts. During the Tang and Song Dynasties, an increasing number of
Kunlun/blacks appeared in the literature, and were usually described
as honest, brave, strong, willing to help others, or with some special
skills, reflecting the reality at the time.

The blacks comprised a large group who settled down in various
places in the world, including Africa, south India, the islands of the
Indian Ocean, and Pacific Ocean, but there is no reason to confirm
that the blacks in China had only one origin. When Arabia sent
its delegation headed by its ambassador to China in 977 CE, "their
attendants had sunken eyes and black skin and they were called *Kunlun nu*," according to History of the Song Dynasty. The blacks here
could be from Africa. As for those of Indian origin, there were two
groups of Negroid. One is known as the "black untouchables" who
as the indigenous inhabitants contributed a great deal to the civilization of the Indus River Valley.[13] The other comprises those who
migrated by themselves to India or were brought by Arabs or Indians
from East Africa as slaves (Rashidi, 1995: 65-120). The third origin
is Southeast Asia, which many works have mentioned, with Ge's as
representative of this group (Ge, 2001). Another view considers that
the blacks of the Han and Tang Dynasties were from Southeast Asia
and East Africa respectively (Hu & Zhang, 1961).

Regarding the origin of the blacks in the Tang period, Zhang
points to Africa and Ge suggests Southeast Asia, a kind of "singular
origin." After examining both arguments, although with rich materials and sound logic, each however emphasized the positive evidence
while neglecting materials negative to their view. Zhang stressed that

the blacks were brought by Arabs, yet ignored those from Zhenla (present-day Cambodia) or Keling (present-day Java). Ge made the same mistake by stressing that the blacks were from Nan Hai yet lost sight of the slaves brought by the Arabs. Historical research should be more careful and open the room for alternative explanation. In sum, multiple origins might be a more reasonable and convincing answer to the question (Li, 1982).

Were the blacks all slaves in ancient China? This is a very sensitive or even provocative question. The question is raised here for three reasons. First, a common impression among the Chinese is that the blacks were mainly slaves (especially during the Tang period) owing to several reasons, including the influence of Zhang's work. Secondly, several recently published works in English suggest the same view with titles like "Magical Kunlun and 'Devil Slaves'" (Wilensky, 2002), or "The Slaves of Guangzhou," the title of a major chapter in *The Blacks in Premodern China* (Wyatt, 2010). Wyatt's book "bolsters a conceptualization of African history and of Africa's historical connections with the rest of the world as a history of slavery," which is always "defined by master-slave relations" (Bodomo, 2013).[14] Thirdly, as Runoko Rashidi correctly points out, "The story of the African presence in early Asia would be incomplete without the expose of the black role as servant or slave" (Rashidi, 1995). An objective answer to the question can provide a more comprehensive picture of their life and work at the time. It is found that besides slaves and servants, the blacks served as soldiers or military leaders, royal guards, government officials, traders, artists, animal trainers and laborers in ancient China.

Since various pieces of literature of the Tang Dynasty and beyond illustrate that some of the blacks were *nubi* (slave-servant), there is no doubt that being domestic servants was one of their major roles. Wyatt did make a comparison at one point: "The perceptible cultural shortcomings that all *kunlun*, regardless of breed, exhibited had the effect only of encouraging Chinese designs on their enslavement and reinforcing the moral legitimacy of the practice as beneficial to the enslaved, much in the same way that the 'white man's burden' premise justified the most egregious imperialist actions whereby

Victorian Britons subjugated millions of people of color around the globe in the nineteenth century" (Wyatt, 2010: 41). This comparison is inadequate, since there was a world of difference between Chinese and British systems of enslavement. It is beyond this chapter to study the issue, yet Joseph Needham expressed his understanding of the difference as follows: "The Chinese and other Asian nations had been using negro slaves for many centuries, but the fact that their slavery was basically domestic kept the practice within bounds short of the massive imports for plantation labor that dominated the Atlantic Trade" (Needham, 1971). Bodomo points out that although Africans and Chinese met a long time ago, they were "on equal footing for the most part, and Africans and Chinese never owned each other as slaves on any large scale or in any systematic manner" (Bodomo, 2012, 2013). What is more, as early as the Tang Dynasty, several emperors issued orders to prohibit the trade in slaves (Schafer, 1963: 45). The Chinese government prohibited the trade of Chinese women by foreigners in 1614, because of a serious problem caused by European slave traders in the coastal regions of China.

Juyan Hanjian indicates that quite a few blacks in the army became officials, nobilities, or border officers. Among 53 blacks, 16 had the rank of nobility, including four officials, and the highest rank being the first class (Zhang, 1977). Blacks also became members of the retinue of royal families or even the emperor. *Song Shu* recorded that Emperor Xiaowu (454-465 CE) trusted a *Kunlun* named Baizhu who was often ordered to cane the officials. The Asian Art Museum in San Francisco possesses a fourteenth century Chinese painting of a black official, obviously of a high rank judged by his costume and bearing (Rashidi, 1995: 141). A famous artist, Liu Guangdao, has a painting, "Yuan Shizhu's Hunting" (1280 CE), which portrayed Emperor Kublai Khan on a hunting expedition. As part of the painting, Emperor and Empress with two attendants, with a black person on horse on the Emperor's left side, was present. He must have been an important military officer or a personal guard. Some blacks also served in the army. When the Dutch invaded Taiwan, Africans were among both the Dutch army and the Chinese army.

Figure 3: Liu Guangdao's painting "Yuan Shizhu's hunting"
(1280 CE).

Some blacks or Africans were merchants in China. When Ibn Battuta visited China, he met his country-fellow doing business in China who "had about fifty white slaves and as many slave girls, and presented me with two of each" (Ibn Battuta, 1929). Gaafar Ahmed, a post-doctoral student in Peking University, did research on the contact between the Sudan and China and found that there is a long history of business between the Sudan and China. In his interview with Ahmed Salih Sabit, he found Salih's grandmother to be a Chinese who went to the Sudan with her husband Mohamed al-Haj, who did business in China for several years (Ahmed 1987, 1999). Blacks in China worked as actors, musicians, acrobats, wild animal trainers, porters, and peasants. European encounter with China also brought African slaves to the coastal regions. An increasing number of Africans served as porters, guards, soldiers, and domestic attendants in foreigners' residence or in the coastal areas in China (Ai, 1989). Zhu Wan, an official of the Ming Dynasty (1368-1644), indicated in his work *Pi Yu Zaji* that Africans were used in the Portuguese army in the colonial occupation of Macao; the Chinese army once captured more than 60 soldiers in a battle and three of them were from Morocco, Ethiopia, and Sudan, respectively. In the fight against the Dutch army in Taiwan, African soldiers were in the Chinese army led by Zheng Chenggong during the Ming period.

AFRICAN DIASPORA IN CONTEMPORARY CHINA: OPPORTUNITY AND CHALLENGE

Owing to the rapid development of China-Africa relations, the African diaspora in China became a hot topic in international academia. Since a survey on Africans in China was only recently published (Bodomo, 2014), I will discuss the topic very briefly and emphasize other issues the survey did not cover, such as special contributions and African students in China. I will also examine the works by Chinese scholars with which international academia is less familiar.

Various African social groups exist in China such as traders, diplomats, artists, students, and professionals. The African trader is by far the largest which aroused great interest among the international community. Studies generally focus on African trading communities in China (Bertoncello & Bredeloup, 2006, 2009; Bodomo, 2007, 2009c, 2012; Bertoncello, Bredeloup & Pliez, 2009; Ditgen, 2010; Cissé, 2013) or their economic practice in Guangzhou, a city hosting the largest group of Africans (Bertoncello & Bredeloup, 2007a, 2007b; Bodomo, 2010; Lyons et al, 2008, 2012, 2013; Li et al, 2008, 2009a, 2009b, 2012; Osnos, 2009; Li & Du, 2012a, 2012b; Bodomo & Ma, 2010; Diederich, 2010; Bork et al, 2011; Müller, 2011; Haugen, 2012; Bredeloup, 2012; Yang, 2013) and Yiwu, the biggest center of commodities in China (Le Bail, 2009; Bertoncello, Bredeloup & Pliez, 2009; Pliez, 2010; Bodomo & Ma, 2010, 2012; Ma 2012), and their business negotiations and deals in Hong Kong (Bodomo, 2007, 2012; Ho, 2012; Mathews, 2000; Mathews & Yang, 2012) and Macau (Morais, 2009; Bodomo, 2012; Bodomo & Silva, 2012). Other researches include the living conditions, social practices or religious activities of the African diaspora (Li et al, 2008, 2009a, 2009b; Li & Du, 2012a, 2012b; Bertoncello & Bredeloup, 2009; Bodomo, 2009a, 2010; Xu, 2009a, 2009b; Yang, 2011; Müller, 2011; Haugen, 2013b), difficulties between Africans and Chinese, management of the African diaspora by the Chinese authorities or the reaction of Chinese citizens (Li and Du,

2012b; Xu,2009a; Osnos, 2009; Morais, 2009; Bodomo, 2010; Haugen, 2012). The African entrepreneurs' role in transmitting their conceptualization of China to their own countries explains the impact of Chinese development in a global context (Marfaing & Thiel, 2014; Cissé, 2013). A cyber network TADIA (The African Diaspora in Asia) was established to bring together scholars of different disciplines, and it is recognized as a project associated with UNESCO (Jayasuriya and Pierre-Angenot, 2006).

Among scholars of the African diaspora in China, two are prominent, Adams Bodomo and Li Zhigang. Bodomo made the best use of his experience in Hong Kong for more than ten years and studied the African diaspora in China, covering various aspects. His training as a linguist offered him the sensitivity about language, food and the life styles of diasporic groups. Being an African provided him convenience to contact African diaspora members in different cities in China; he published extensively on the subject. Bodomo's important contribution lies in his "immigrant community as bridge" theory. Since the "push-pull" theory first appeared in 1959, it has been well received in academia. Yet this is a 'double-end' approach, which neglects the process itself and the immigrants' role after their arrival.[15] By using a three-dimensional approach that recognizes the target community, its source community and its host community, Bodomo put forward the "immigrant community as bridge" theory, suggesting that given the right conditions, the target community can serve "as a bridge—connecting its place of origin (its source community) with its new place of domicile (its host community)" (Bodomo, 2010, 2012).

Li Zhigang has focused on the African community in Guangzhou. As an expert on urban and human geography, Li places China's African diaspora in the context of economic globalization and transnational migration. Using the theoretical framework of "enclave" in migration studies, Li analyzes the development of "ethnic economic enclave" with double-character, high mobility and diversity on one hand and high possibility of residential segregation on the other (Li et al., 2008). The enclave includes three circles of social ties: the core of African traders, circled by their communities,

and the third, so-called China-Africa circle of the interactions between Africans and local Chinese, which forms a part of the process
of globalization. The social space and networks under transnational
entrepreneurialism mark the coming of a new era of globalization in
urban China, providing opportunity and challenge for local government (Li et al, 2009; Li & Du, 2011). The most impressive feature
of his study lies in the approach of taking the "ethnic economic enclave" as a historical process, forming and transforming constantly,
not just a pattern.

Sociologist Xu Tao's works emphasizes social adaptation of
African merchants in Guangzhou and found them to have multiple
features of social relations. Concentrated or dispersed, their adaptation takes three forms—individual, re-socialization, and network
with various supportive measures. The characteristic of the African
diaspora is one of coexistence in heterogeneity, and an international
community emerging (Xu 2009a, 2011, 2012, 2013).

Ma Enyu's study focuses on the African community in Yiwu,
analyzing its change from a small town to an internationally well-
known commercial hub and its role in China-Africa relations (Ma
2010, 2012; Bodomo & Ma, 2010, 2012). A comparison between
an international community in Yiwu and the African community
in Guangzhou indicates various differences, especially of social capital (Chen, 2012). The theory of social support is applied to analyze
the extent, role and impact of social support on or social capital of
the African diaspora in Guangzhou (Xu, 2009b; Chen, 2012). It is
noticed that the media played an important role in formulating the
image of Africans in Guangzhou, and with more contact, the more
positive the view towards the Africans (Li et al, 2009). British coverage on immigrants and its strategy is discussed in order to provide a
lesson for Chinese media in the coverage of the African diaspora in
China (Dang, 2013).

The above-mentioned works have several features in common.
They are the fruits of fieldwork and the data collected in
Guangzhou, Hong Kong or Yiwu. Second, most of the works are
project and reality-based research either as a result of or an explanation for the fast development of China-Africa relations. Thirdly,

the influential works are usually conducted through team-based research, which includes African, Chinese, or European partners. The African diaspora is characterized by its full engagement in the economy of their host cities and by poor social integration, caused by lack of communication, misunderstanding, strict immigration policy, cultural difference and a lack of religion in the Chinese society. Whether there is racism in China, there seems to be different views.[16]

Although most international students are not classified as immigrants, Bodomo correctly pointed out that the process of trade between Africa and China began with Africans who studied in China and remained there to do business (Bodomo, 2013). After African countries won their independence, they started to send African students or technicians to China for advanced studies. Students from 14 African countries regularly came to China till the end of 1966, when China closed all universities because of the Cultural Revolution. Among them, a Ghanaian student Immanuel Hevi complained about racism and other unpleasant phenomena in China (Hevi, 1963; Liu, 2013). From Ghana, where President Nkrumah was strongly pro-socialist, Hevi's negative story about China behind the iron curtain brought about applause from Western analysts, who were looking for ammunition against China and his book provided one. Yet Hevi's complaint was understandable for several reasons. In the early 1960s, China witnessed its most difficult time in its economy and could not have provided any better conditions to the students. Social taboos and regulations set up a kind of "segregation" between African males and Chinese females, plus the pervasive politics of the time (Li & Liu, 2013).

China resumed educational cooperation with Africa in 1972 and trainees of railway technology came from Tanzania and Zambia first, then regular students followed in 1973. African students in China in 1973-1976 numbered 355. With an increasing number, problems occurred, and the racial tension broke out at the end of the 1980s when African and Chinese students both held demonstrations and accused each other of various wrongs (Sautman, 1994). From today's perspective, cultural differences seem to be a major cause, since the

trigger was usually the close contact between African male students
and Chinese girls (Li & Liu, 2013). With the set-up of the Forum
on China-Africa Cooperation (FOCAC), the number of African students greatly increased.[17] The first studies on the issue in China were
by scholars at the Center for African Studies at Peking University
based on the archives of the Ministry of Education, with the focus
on African students in China (Editorial Group, 2005; Li Baoping,
2006, 2013).

Studies on the topic focus on four subjects—cultural adaptation,
China-Africa cooperation, student management, and language
teaching.[18] Psychology is often applied in cross-cultural research and
two works are worth mentioning. One is an article based on SASS
(Study Abroad Stress Survey) of Africans and westerners. It indicates
that academic and interpersonal sources of stress were the most common and daily hassles defined as high pressure and challenge among
both males and females.[19] Another psychological study found that
all African students experienced a culture shock in China, more serious for undergraduates than graduates, females than males.[20] Other
studies are either on cultural adaptation (Yi & Xiong, 2013; Gong,
2014), cultural difference and its impact (Long & Xiong, 2014)
or different concepts of time and family (Ye Shuai, 2011). As for
the role in China-Africa cooperation, Ketema found that there is
an important role for Chinese universities in China-Africa cooperation (Ketema Meskela et al, 2009), King saw the presence of African
students in China as an indicator of China's soft power (King,
2012), Haugen analyzed China's policy for enrolment of African
students and its effect and outcome (Haugen, 2013a), while others
argued that China's educational assistance formed an essential part of
China-Africa cooperation and offered substantial support to Africa
(Li, 2006; Li & Luo, 2013; Xu, 2007; He, 2007; Lou & Xu, 2012).
Studies also focused on the management of African students in China, either in universities or in society (Cheng, 2012; Zheng, 2012,
2013a, 2013b; An et al., 2014). The fourth subject always involves
language teachers who are looking for a better way to teach Chinese languages (Lin & Ren, 2010). There are common features of
these studies—cross-cultural theory with questionnaires as method-

ology and concrete suggestions provided. The short-coming here is that these studies are usually based on a case-study of African students in a place (or a university) or from a country, thus limitations are inevitable. How to apply these theories in case studies is another problem. However, with a rapid increase of African students in China, this remains an important topic of study (Li, 2014b).

CONCLUSION

Since the title of this chapter covers a wide range, the limitation of it is obvious. It should be taken as an "opening-remark" rather than a "conclusion." It indicates that there are various issues in China-Africa relations, be it historical or contemporary, or in different disciplines. The bilateral migration provides both opportunity and challenge. There are cultural similarities and differences between China and Africa and mutual learning is always beneficial to both (Li, 2012b, 2014a). There is still a lack of solid studies on the topic. How do we carry out research on the historical links between Africans and Chinese? What is the best way to build the linkage between the two cultures, thus to facilitate the transfer process from "enclave" to "bridge"? How do we promote the efficiency of African talents as they study in China with the hope of promoting African development? Why is there a gap between the African diaspora and local communities in China and how do we narrow this gap? How can we manage intermarriages and increasingly mixed groups of children, and who should be in charge of the African community, the Chinese authorities or African community leaders, or a combined team? Is it necessary to give up one's own culture and adapt to another, or is there a better way for diasporic communities to keep their own culture and fit in the host society? All these questions are relevant for Chinese communities in Africa as well.

My view regarding China-Africa relations is unique: the more problems, the better. Why? The reason is simple: no contact, no problem. When contacts get wider and deeper, of course there are bound to be more problems. China and Africa are on equal footing trying to solve their problems. As each problem gets solved, the relationship gets closer.

REFERENCES

"African communities in China hail Xi's visit," *China Daily*, March 24, 2013.

"African community needs more attention," *China Daily*, November 2, 2009.

"Africans create community in Guangzhou," *China Daily*, October 14, 2013.

African Union (2005) Report of the meeting of experts from the members of the States on the Definition of African Diaspora, April 11-12, Addis Ababa, Ethiopia.

Ahmed, Gaafar Karrar (1999). Sino-Arab Relations during Tang Dynasty 618-CE, *Tang Studies*, Vol.5, 323-366.

Ahmed, Gaafar Karrar (1999) Sudan-China relations during the Tang Dynasty to the end of Yuan Dynasty. *Yuanshi Luncong*, No.7, Nanchang: Jiangxi jiaoyu chubanshe, 197-206.

Ai Zhouchang (1987) A survey of the African blacks coming to China, *West Asia and Africa*, No.3,49-55,82.

Ai Zhouchang. ed. (1989) *Zhongfei Guanxishi Wenxian (1500-1918)* (Selection of Materials on Sino-African Relations (1500-1918), Shanghai: Huadong shifan daxue chubanshe.

Alpers, Edward A. (1997) The African Diaspora in the Northwestern Indian Ocean: reconsideration of an old problem, new directions for research," Comparative Studies of South Asia, Africa & the Middle East, 17(2), 62-81.

Alpers, Edward A. (2000) Recollecting Africa: Diasporic memory in the Indian Ocean world," African Studies Review, 43(1), 83-99.

An Ran, et al. (2007) Feizhou liuxuesheng de jiaoyu xuqiu yu zhaosheng xuanchuan muoshi, *High Education Exploration*, 5, 110-113.

Bagne, D.J. (1969) *Principles of Demography*, New York, 1969.

Baitie, Zahra (2013) On Being African in China. *The Atlantic*, August 28, 2013.

Beachey, R.W. (1976) *The Slave Trade of Eastern Africa*, New York: Harper and Row.

Bertoncello, Brigite & Sylvie Bredeloup (2006) La migration chinoise en Afrique: accélérateur du développement ou "sanglot de l'homme noir." *Afrique Contemporaine*, 218, 199–224.

Bertoncello, Brigite & Sylvie Bredeloup (2007a) De Hong Kong à Guangzhou, de nouveaux 'comptoirs' africains s'organisent, *Perspectives chinoises* 98(1), 98–110.

Bertoncello, B. & Sylvie Bredeloup (2007b) The emergence of new African "Trading posts" in Hong Kong and Guangzhou. *China Perspectives*, No.1, 94 -105.

Bertoncello, Brigite & Sylvie Bredeloup (2009) Chine-Afrique ou la valse des entrepreneurs-migrants." *Revue européenne des migrations internationales* 25(1), 45–70.

Bertoncello, Brigite, Sylvie Bredeloup & Olivier Pliez (2009) Hong Kong, Guangzhou, Yiwu: de nouveaux comptoirs africains en Chine. *Critique internationale* 44, 105–121.

Bodomo, A. (2007) An Emerging African-Chinese Community in Hong Kong: The Case of TsimShaTsui's Chungking Mansions, In Kwesi Kwaa Prah, ed., *Afro-Chinese Relations: Past, Present and Future*. Cape Town: Center for Advanced Studies in African Societies.

Bodomo, A. (2009a) Africa-China Relations in an era of globalization: the role of African trading communities in China, *West Asia and Africa*, No. 8, 2009, 62-67.

Bodomo, A. (2009b) Africa-China relations: symmetry, soft power, and South Africa. *The China Review: An Interdisciplinary Journal on Greater China*, 9(2), 2009, 169-178

Bodomo, A. (2009c) The African Presence in Contemporary China.*China Monitor*, January 2009 University of Stellenbosch, South Africa.

Bodomo, A. (2010) The African trading community in Guangzhou: an emerging bridge for Africa-China relations. *The China Quarterly*. 203, 693 – 707

Bodomo, A. (2012) *Africans in China: A Sociocultural Study and Its Implications for Africa-China Relations.* Amherst, New York: Cambria Press.

Bodomo, A. (2013) African diaspora remittances are better than foreign aid funds. *World Economics* (Henley-on-Thames, England), 14(4), 21-28.

Bodomo, A. (2013) Review of Don Wyatt's *The Blacks of Premodern China*, *African Studies Review*, 56, 244-246.

Bodomo, A. (2014) Africans in China: A bibliographical survey, *Annual Review of African Studies in China.2013*, Social Sciences Academic Press, 109-121.

Bodomo, A. & Grace Ma (2010) From Guangzhou to Yiwu: Emerging facets of the African diaspora in China. *International Journal of African Renaissance Studies* 5(2), 283-289.

Bodomo, A. & Grace Ma (2012) We are what we eat: food in the process of community formation and identity shaping among African traders in Guangzhou and Yiwu. *African Diaspora* 5(1), 1-26.

Bodomo, A. & Roberval Silva (2012) Language matters: the role of linguistic identity in the establishment of the lusophone African community in Macau. *African Studies,* 71(1), 71-90.

Bogue, D.J. (1959) International migration. In P. Hauser & O. D. Duncun, eds., *The Study of Population,* Chicago: University of Chicago Press.

Bork, T., et al. (2011) Global Change, National Development Goals, Urbanization and International Migration in China: African Migrants in Guangzhou and Foshan. In F. Kraas, S. Aggarwal, M. Coy & G. Mertins (eds). *Megacities: Our Global Urban Future.* London: Springer.

Bredeloup, S. (2012) African trading posts in Guangzhou: emergent or recurrent commercial form? *African Diaspora* 5(1): 27 – 50.

Broomball, Marshal (1919) *Islam in China, a Neglected Problem,* London: Morgan and Scotts.

Brunson, James (1985) African presence in early China, *Journal of African Civilizations,* 1,121-137.

Cen Zhongmian (1935) Chinese sea route in Tang dynasty: from Persian Gulf to East Africa, *Dongfang Zazhi* (Oriental Miscellany), 41:18.

Chang Kwang Chih (1968[1963]) *The Archaeology of Ancient China,* Yale University Press.

Chen Jianwen (1993) The name and ethnicity of *Rouzhi* and the issue of blacks in border regions of Han Dynasty, *Guoji Jiandu Xuehui Huikan,* No.1, Taibei: Lantai chubanshe.

Cheng Tao, ed. (2013) *Chinese Ambassadors Telling African Stories,* World Affairs Press.

Cheng Weihua, et al. (2012) Feizhou lai hua liuxue yanjiusheng jiaoyu wenti yu duice, *Degree and Graduate Research.* 8, 54-58.

Chen Yupeng (2012) Shehui ziben yu chengshi waiguoren shequ de xingcheng, *Forward Position,* 4, 114-115.

Cheng Guofu (2002) An Examination on the Phenomenon of the Kunlun Slaves of Tang Dynasty *Journal of Jinan University(Philosophy & Social Science Edition),* 24(5), 79-84.

China Africa Project (2013) Leading China scholar Li Anshan recalls his experiences teaching African students, http://www.chinaafricaproject.com/leading-china-scholar-li-anshan-recalls-his-experiences-teaching-african-students-translation/.

Chou Yi Liang (1972) Early contacts between China and Africa, *Ghana Notes and Queries*, 12(6), 1-3.

Cissé, Daouda (2013) South-South migration and trade: African traders in China. Policy Briefing, Center for Chinese studies n° 4 / 2013.

Cui Kuai, et al. (2009) Study on the trade pattern of African community in Guangzhou, *Economic Outlook the Bohai Sea*, 5, 14-17.

Dang Fangli (2013) British media's coverage of immigrants and its enlightenment to Chinese media: Basing on the event of Africans' protest in Guangzhou, *Tangdu Journal*, 29(5), 82-86.

Dart, Raymond (1925) Historical succession of cultural impacts upon South Africa, *Nature*, March 21, vol. 115, no. 2890, 425-429.

Dart, Raymond (1939) A Chinese character as a wall motive in Rhodesia, South African Journal of Science, Vol.36, 474-476.

Davies, Carole Elizabeth Boyce (2008) Encyclopedia of the African Diaspora: Origins, Experiences and Culture, ABC-CLIO, Inc.

Diederich, Manon (2010) Manoeuvring through the spaces of everyday life. Transnational experiences of African women in Guangzhou, China. Dissertation at the University of Cologne, Department of Geography.

Dikotter, Frank (1992) *The Discourse of Race in Modern China*. London: C. Hurst and Co.

Disima (2004) Cultural adaptation of foreign students in China, M.A. thesis of psychology, Nanjing Normal University.

Dittgen, Romain (2010) L'Afrique en Chine: l'autre face des relations sino-africaines?" Economie, China Institute. Online, accessed September 2013 http://www.china-institute.org/articles/ L_Afrique_en_Chine_l_autre_face_des_relations_sino_africaines.pdf .

Du Baoren (1979) African black pottery figure in Tang tomb of Xi-an. *Wen Wu*, 6, 88-90.

Duyvendak, J.J.L. (1949) *China's Discovery of Africa*. London: A.Probsthain.

Editorial Group (2005) *China Africa Education Cooperation*, Peking University Press.

Filesi, Teobaldo (Trans. David L. Morison) (1972) *China and Africa in the Middle Ages*, London: Frank Cass.

Freeman-Grenville, G.S.P. (1959) Some problems of East African coinage from early times to 1890, *Tanganyika Notes and Records*, Dar Es Salaam, 53, 250-260.

Ge Chengyong (2001) On the origin of blacks in the Tang Dynasty ' *Zhonghua Wenshi Luncong*, Issue 65, 1-27.

Giese, Karsten & Laurence Marfaing (eds) (2015) Entrepreneurs africains et chinois. Les impacts sociaux d'une rencontre particulière, Paris : Karthala.

Gong Sujuan (2014) Lai hua Feizhou liuxuesheng de kuawenhua shiying yanjiu, *Journal of Kaifeng Institute of Education* ' 34(2), 127-130.

Goodrich, L.C. (1931) Negroes in China, *Bulletin of the Catholic University of Peking*, 8, 137-39.

Guangzhou Shi Wenwu Guanli Weiyuanhui Deng. 1981. *Tombs of the Han in Guangzhou* (1), Wenwu Publishers.

Hamdun, Said & Noel King (1975) *Ibn Battuta in Black Africa*, London: Rex Collings.

Han, H. (2013) Individual Grassroots Multilingualism in Africa Town in Guangzhou: The Role of States in globalization. *International Multilingual Research Journal* 7(1), 83-97.

Han Huamei (2014) Guangzhou Feizhoucheng de caogen duoyu zhuyi: guojia zai quanqiuhua zhong banyan de juese, *Annual Review of African Studies in China.2013*, Social Sciences Academic Press, 86-108.

Harris, Joseph E. ed. (1993) *Global Dimensions of the African Diaspora*, 2nd ed. Washington, DC: Howard University Press.

Hashim, I. H., & Z. L. Yang (2003) Cultural and gender differences in perceiving stressors: a cross-cultural investigation of African and Western students in Chinese colleges. *Stress and Health,*19 (4), 217-225.

Hashim, Ismail Hussein et al. (2003) Cultural and gender differences in perceiving Stressors: A crosscultural investigation of African and Western Students at Chinese Colleges, *Psychological Science*, 26(5), 795-799.

Haugen, H. Ø. (2011) Chinese exports to Africa: Competition, complementarity and cooperation between micro-level actors. *Forum for Development Studies* 38(2), 157-176.

Haugen, H. Ø. (2012) Nigerians in China: A second state of immobility. *International Migration*, 50 (2), 65-80.

Haugen, H. Ø (2013a) China's recruitment of African university students: policy efficacy and unintended outcomes. *Globalisation, Societies and Education,*11(3), 315-334.

Haugen, H. Ø (2013b) African pentecostal migrants in China: Marginalization and the alternative geography of a mission theology. *African Studies Review.* 56(1), 81-102.

He Wenping (2007) A summary analysis of China-Africa educational exchanges and cooperation : development phases and challenges, *West Asia and Africa,* 3. 13-18.

Hevi, Emmanuel (1963) *An African Student in China.* Pall Mall.

Ho, W.-Y. (2013) Mobilizing the Muslim minority for China's development: Hui Muslims, ethnic relations and Sino-Arab connections. *Journal of Comparative Asian Development,* 12(1), 84-112.

Hu zhaochun & Zhang Weichi (1961) Black pottery figures of the Han Dynasty unearthed in Guangzhou. *Journal of Sun Yatsen University,* 2, 84-87.

Ibn Battuta (1929) (Trans. and selected by H.A.R.Gibb). *Ibn Battuta Travels in Asia and Africa (1325-1354).* 1999, Delhi: LPP.

Jayasuriya, Shihan de Silve & Jean Pierre-Angenot (2006) The African Diaspora in Asia: Historical Gleanings, *Asian and African Studies,* 5:3-4.

Jing Zhaoxi (1998) On coming of African blacks to China during the Tang Dynaty. *Xibei Di Er Minzu Xueyuan Xuebao,* No.4, 51-54.

Ketema Meskela, et al. (2009) The research on educational cooperation between China and Africa: An African perspective, *Studies in Foreign Education,* 36(1), 50-53.

King, Kenneth (2013) *China's Aid and Soft Power in Africa,* James Currey.

Lacouperie, Terrien de (1887) *The Languages of China before the Chinese,* London: David Nutt.

Le Bail, Hélène (2009) Les grandes villes chinoises comme espace d'immigration internationale: le cas des entrepreneurs africains. *Asie Visions* 19.

Li Anshan (2000) *A History of Overseas Chinese in Africa,* Chinese Overseas Publishing House.

Li Anshan (2005) African studies in China in the Twentieth Century: A Historiographical Survey. *African Studies Review* 48(1), 59-87.

Li Anshan (2006) *Social History of Chinese Overseas in Africa, Selected Documents (1800-2005),* Hong Kong Press for Social Sciences Ltd.

Li Anshan (2008) Gli studi africanistici in Cina agli inizi del XXI secolo. *Afriche e Orienti,* No.2, as part of the dossier, Cristiana Fiamingo, ed., *La Cina in Africa.*

Li Anshan (2010) African Studies in China : A Historiographical Survey, in Harneit-Sievers, Alex et al., eds., *Chinese and African Perspectives on China in Africa*, Pambazuka Press, 2-24.

Li Anshan (2012a) *A History of Overseas Chinese in Africa to 1911*. NY: Diasporic Africa Press.

Li Anshan (2012b) China and Africa: cultural similarity and mutual learning. In James Shikwati, ed., *China-African Partnership-The quest for a win-win relationship*, Nairobi: Inter Region Economic Network.

Li Anshan (2013) My African students. In Cheng Tao & Lu Miaogen, eds., *Chinese Ambassadors Tell African Stories*, World Affairs Press.

Li Anshan (2014a) Similarities between Chinese culture and African culture—With reference to what China can learn from Africa. *West Asia and Africa*, 1, 49-63.

Li Anshan (2014b) A place to learn, a place to realize dreams, *China Daily*, April, 11, 2014. http://www.chinadaily.com.cn/world/2014livisitafrica/2014-04/11/content_17477854.htm.

Li Anshan & Liu Haifang (2013) The evolution of the Chinese policy of funding African students and an evaluation of the effectiveness. Draft report for UNDP. CAS at Peking University.

Li Baoping (2006) China-Africa educational cooperation and intellectual assistance to Africa, http://www.cpaffc.org.cn/c06/yw20020904.html

Li Baoping & Luo Jianbo (2013) Dissecting soft power and Sino-Africa relations in education and exchanges cooperation. In Li Anshan & Funeka Yazini April. *Forum on China-Africa Cooperation: The Politics of Human Resources Development*, AIAS.

Li Chi (1928) *The Formation of the Chinese People*, Harvard University Press.

Li Jiping (1982) Examination of Kunlun slaves in the Tang Dynasty, *Wenshi*, 6, 98-118.

Li Jiangtao & Li Xiang (2006) China is my second hometown: African students' life in Beijing. http://news.xinhuanet.com/world/2006-10/21/content_5232813.htm

Li Xinfeng (2013) *Feizhou ta xun Zheng He lu* (Seek Zheng He's Passage in Africa). China Social Sciences Press.

Li Zhigang, et al. (2008) The African enclave of Guangzhou: A case study of Xiaobeilu, 63(2), *ACTA Geographica Sinica*.

Li Zhigang, et al. (2009a) The local response of transnational social space under globalization in urban China: A case study of African enclave in Guangzhou, *Geographical Research*, 28(4), 920-932.

Li Zhigang, et al. (2009b) An African enclave in China: The making of a new transnational urban space. *Eurasian Geography and Economics* 50(6), 699 – 719.

Li Zhigang & Du Feng (2012a) Production of China's new social space in city under "transnational entrepreneurialism" A case study on African economic zone in Guangzhou, *Urban Space Studies*, 36(8), 25-31.

Li Zhigang & Du Feng (2012b) The transnational making of "Chocolate City" in Guangzhou. *Renwen Dili* 27(6), 1-6.

Li Zhigang, et al. (2012) China's 'Chocolate City': An Ethnic Enclave in a Changing Landscape, *African Diaspora*, 5, 51-72.

Liang Jingwen (2004) A study on Kunlun nu in the Tang Dynasty, *Maritime History Studies*, 2.58-62.

Lin Lunlun & Ren Mengya (2010) A socioliguistic study upon Chinese language learning concept of African overseas students, *Journal of Hanshan Normal University*, 31 (5), 32-37.

Ling Shun-sheng (1956) Negritoes in Chinese History, *Annals of Academia Sinica*, 3, 251-267.

Liu, P. H. (2013) Petty annoyances? Revisiting John Emmanuel Hevi's *An African Student in China* after 50 years. *An International Journal.* 11(1), 131-145.

Lokongo, Antoine Roger (2012) My Chinese connection. *CHINAFRICA*, July, 50.

Long Xia & Xiong Lijun (2014) The influence of Sino-African cultural difference on the education of African students in China: taking Angola students as the example, *Journal of Chongqing University of Education*, 27(1), 133-136.

Lou Shizhou & Xu Hui (2012) The development and transition of China-Africa educational cooperation in the new period, *Educational Research*, 10, 28-33.

Lyons, M., A. Brown, & Li Zhigang (2008) The 'third tier' of globalization: African traders in Guangzhou. *City*, 12(2), 196-206

Ly-Tio-Fane-Pineo, Huguette (1981) *La Diaspora Chinoise dans L'OceanIndien Occidental* ﹐ Aix-en-Provence: Association des Chercheurs de l'Ocean d'Indien, Institut d'Histoire des pays d'Outre-mer, Greco Ocean Indien.

Ly-Tio-Fane-Pineo, Huguette (1985) *The Chinese Diaspora of the Western Indian Ocean*, Éditions de l'océan Indien.

Ly-Tio-Fane Pineo, Huguette & Edouard Lim Fat (2008) *From Alien to Citizen: the Integration of the Chinese in Mauritius*. Éditions de l'océan Indien.

Lyons, M., A. Brown & Li Zhigang (2012) In the dragon's den: African traders in Guangzhou. *Journal of Ethnic and Migration Studies*, 38(5), 869-888.

Lyons, M., Alison Brown & Li Zhigang (2013) The China-Africa Value Chain: Can Africa's Small-Scale Entrepreneurs Engage Successfully in Global Trade? *African Studies Review*, 56(3), 77-100.

Ma Enyu (2010) Walking into the Yiwu Muslim community, *China Religion*, 6, 56-57.

Ma Enyu (2012) Yiwu mode and Sino-African relations. *Journal of Cambridge Studies*,7(3), 93-108.

Ma Wenkuan & Meng Fanren (1987) Zhongguo Guci zai Feizhou de Faxian (The Discovery of Chinese ancient porcelains in Africa), Beijing: Forbidden City Press.

Mandela, Winnie, ed. A. Benjamin & M. Benson (1985) *Part of My Soul Went with Him*, Norton.

Marfaing, Laurence & Alena Thiel (2014) *"Agents of Translation": West African Entrepreneurs in China as Vectors of Social Change*, Working Paper, No.4, DFG Priority Program 1448, http://www.spp1448.de/fileadmin/media/galleries/SPP_Administration/Working_Paper_Series/SPP1448_WP4_Marfaing-Thiel_final.pdf

Marsh, Jenni (2014) Afro-Chinese marriages boom in Guangzhou: but will it be 'til death do us part'?June 1, http://www.scmp.com/magazines/post-magazine/article/1521076/afro-chinese-marriages-boom-guangzhou-will-it-be-til-death (Retrieved 6/24/2014)

Mathews, G. (2000) "Les traders africains a Kong Hong (Hong Kong) et en Chine," *Les Temps Modernes*, no.657 (Janvier-mars, 2000), 110-124.

Mathews, G. & Yang, Y. (2012) How Africans pursue low-end globalization in Hong Kong and mainland China. *Journal of Current Chinese Affairs*,41(2), 95-120.

Mohamed, H.E. (1990) *The Golden Age of Africa: Classical Period*, Highlight Publications of Calgary.

Morais, I. (2009) "China wahala": The tribulations of Nigerian "Bushfallers" in a Chinese Territory. *Transtext(e)s Transcultures. Journal of Global Cultural Studies* 5, 1-22.

Müller, A. & R. Wehrhahn (2013) Transnational business networks of African intermediaries in China: Practices of networking and the role of experiential knowledge. *DIE ERDE–Journal of the Geographical Society of Berlin*, 144(1), 82-97.

Müller, Angelo (2011) New Migration Processes in Contemporary China–Te Constitution of African Trader Networks in Guangzhou. *Geographische Zeitschrif* 99(2), 104–122.

Needham, Joseph (1971) *Science and Civilization in China*, 4(3) , Cambridge University Press.

Osnos, Evan. 2009. The Promised Land–Guangzhou's Canaan market and the rise of an African merchant class. *The New Yorker*, February 9.–16. 50–56.

Park, Y. Jung (2008) *A Matter of Honour: Being Chinese in South Africa* Jacana Media (Pty) Ltd.

Pinto, Jeanette (2006) The African native in diaspora, *African and Asian Studies*, 5(3-4), 383-397.

Pliez, O. (2010) Toutes les routes de la soie mènent in Yiwu (Chine). Entrepreneurs et migrants musulmans dans un comptoir économique chinois. *Espace Géographique* 2, 132–145.

Qin Jie (2010) Discovery and research of pottery figures in Han tombs in Guangzhou, MA thesis, Jilin University, 2010.

Rashidi, Runoko (1985) Commentaries, *Journal of African Civilizations*, 1,147-148.

Rashidi, Runoko & Ivan Van Sertima, eds. (2007[1995]) *The African Presence in Early Asia*. New Brunswick: Transaction Press.

Rennie, N. (2009) The lion and the dragon: African experiences in China. *Journal of African Media Studies*.1(3), 379-414.

Sautman, Barry (1994) Anti-Black Racism in Post-Mao China. *The China Quarterly*, 138,413-437.

Schafer, Edward (1963) *The Golden Peaches of Samarkand: A Study of Tang Exotics*. The Regents of the University of California.

Segal, Ronald (2001) *Islam's Black Slaves, The Other Black*, New York: Farrar, Straus and Giroux.

Shen Fuwei (1990) *Zhongguo yu Feizhou: Zhong Fei Guanxi Er Qian Nian* (China and Africa: Relations of 2000 Years), Beijing: Zhonghua shuju.

Shepperson, G. (1993) African diasopra: concept and context. In J. E. Harris, ed. *Global Dimensions of the African Diaspora*, 2nd ed. Washington, DC: Howard University Press, 41-49.

Weidenreich, F. (1939) On the earliest representatives of modern mankind recovered on the soil of East Asia, *Peking Natural History Bulletin*, 13(3), 161-174.

Wyatt, Don J. (2010) *The Blacks of Premodern China*. University. of Pennsylvania Press.

Wong-Hee-Kan, Edith (1996) *La Diaspora Chinoise au Marscareignes: Le cas de la Reunion*. Editions L'Harmattan.

Xu Hui (2007) Sino-Africa educational cooperation under the FOCAC framework, *Educational Development Research*, 9, 1-7.

Xu Tao (2009a) An analysis on Africans social relations and interaction logics in Guangzhou, *Youth Research*, No.5, 71-86.

Xu Tao (2009b) African's social support in Guangzhou: Weakening, fracture and reconstruction, *South China Population*, 24: 4, 34-44.

Xu Tao (2011) Re-analysis of the relations of social contact of African merchants in Guangzhou, *Journal of Zhejiang Normal University*, 4,10-15.

Xu Tao (2012) Analysis of characteristics of the behavior of African merchants in Guangzhou, *Journal of Zhejiang Normal University*, 4, 55-63.

Xu Tao (2013) *The Social Adaptations of African Merchants in China*, Zhejiang Renmin Chubanshe.

Xu Yongzhang (1983) Africans who visited China in ancient times, *History Monthly*, 3, 96-98.

Xu Yongzhang (1984) Africa as recorded in Twenty-four Histories, *Journal of Henan University*, 4, 95-101.

Xu Yongzhang (1980) Africa recorded in ancient Chinese literature, *World History*, 6. 53-61,52.

Yang Ximei (1966) A preliminary report of human crania excavated from Houchia-chuang and other Shang Dynasty sites at An-yang, Honan, North China, *The Annual Bulletin of the China Council for East Asian Studies*, no.5, 1-13.

Yang Ximei (1995) *Xianqin Wenhua Shi Lunji* (Collection on Cultural History in Pre-Qin Period), Beijing: China Social Sciences Press.

Yang Yang (2011) New Silk Roads: African and Chinese traders in South China and South Africa. *The China Monitor* 61: 4–8.

Yang,Y. (2013) African Traders in Guangzhou. In G.Mathews, G.L.Ribero & C.A.Vega eds. *Globalization from Below: The World's Other Economy*, Routledge, Taylor and Francis.

Yap, Melanie Yap & Daniel Leong Man (1996) *Colour, Confusion and Concessions: The History of the Chinese in South Africa.* Hong Kong: Hong Kong University Press.

Ye Shuai (2011) A comparative analysis of the cross-cultural communication based on the Somali students and the Chinese students on time and family concepts, *Kexue Wenhui*, 11, 30-31.

Yi Pei & Xiong Lijun (2013) An empirical study of intercultural adaptation of African students in China, *Journal of Shenyang University (social science)*, 15:3, 364-368.

Zhang Chunshu (1977) *Handai Bianjiang Shi Lunji* (On History of Border of the Han Dynasty) Taibei: Shihuo chuban she.

Zeleza, Paul Tiyambe (2005) Rewriting the African Diaspora: Beyond the Black Atlantic, *African Affairs*, 104:414 (January), 35-68.

Zeleza, Paul Tiyambe (2008) The challenges of studying African diasporas, *African Sociological Review*, 12(2), 4-21.

Zhang Tiesheng. 1963. *Zhong-Fei Jiaotong Shi Chu Tan* (History of Sino-African Relations: A Primary Research), Beijing: Joint Publishing.

Zhang Xiang (1987) "Four high-tides of the contacts between Africa and China in ancient times," *Nakai Shixue* (History in Nankai University), 2.

Zhang Xinglang [Chang Hsinglang] (1928) The importation of African black slaves to China during the Tang. *Furen Xuezhi*, 1, 101-119.

Zhang Xinglang [Chang Hsinglang] (1930) The importation of black slaves to China in Tang Dynasty (618-907), *Bulletin of Catholic University of Peking*, No.7, 37-59.

Zhang Xinglang (Chang Hsinglang), ed., Zhu Jieqing, revised. (1977[1930]) *Zhongxi jiaotong shiliao huibian*, vol.2, Zhonghua shuju.

Zhao Rukuo (1996[1225]) (Collated and annotated by Yang Bowen). *Zhufan Zhi Jiaoshi* (Explanation of Records of Foreign Nations). Beijing: Zhonghua shuju.

Zhu Chun-ting (2004) The western image in the eyes of the Chinese during the Ming and Qing Dynasties, *Journal of Jiangxi Institute of Education (Social Science)*, 25(5), 98-103.

Zheng Jianghua (2012) Research on safety management of African students on university campus, *Journal of Tianjin University of Technology and Education*, 22(4), 72-74.

Zheng Jianghua, et al. (2013a) Construction of community management system for foreign Students in universities, *Vocational and Technical Education*, 34(23), 66-68.

Zheng Jianghua (2013b) Exploration of compound applied talents training mode on African students, *Journal of Tianjin University of Technology and Education*, 23 (4), 64-70.

AFRICAN TRADERS IN YIWU: TRADE NETWORKS AND THE DISTRIBUTION OF "MADE IN CHINA" PRODUCTS IN AFRICA

DAOUDA CISSÉ

INTRODUCTION

With its world economic influence based on trade alongside its modernisation, China is becoming an important economic migration destination. While immigrants in China are attracted to the country because of work and study, a large number of foreigners, mainly Africans, have opted for trade and business. Beside the large number of African traders who travel back and forth from their home countries to China, a growing number of Africans have decided to live, establish themselves and set up businesses in China. Most of them are based in Guangzhou (southern China), which is a trading hub in China's domestic as well as foreign trade due to its location in the Pearl River Delta and its proximity to Hong Kong. Increasingly, Yiwu in eastern China is becoming an important international trading hub with its specialised markets. Local policies to develop markets, infrastructure and transform Yiwu to become a business crossroads in China have been put in place in order to attract traders from all over. China's industrialisation and entrepreneurial reforms have enabled Chinese entrepreneurs to set up factories in southern and eastern China, which supply China's domestic as well as international markets through exports. African traders have been attracted by the "made in China" products with a competitive price manufactured from the factories in Guangdong and around Yiwu.

The trajectory of African traders in China is diverse. While a number of African traders come directly from their home countries to China, others came from other regions of the world (Asia, Europe and North America) where they had established businesses. China's booming trade and the 1997 financial crisis in Asia and lower costs of doing business in China have driven the majority of those traders to relocate to China's city-markets. Even though based in Asia, Europe or North America, they have developed trade networks with their fellow traders in their home countries as well as in other regions of the world. While most of those trade networks were mainly based on social, kinship or religious ties, today they are more driven by business relations and ties. Even though established in China, African traders have developed trade and business ties with traders based in Africa or who travel to and order products from China. Through those established networks, they supply African markets with "made in China" products. This chapter explores African traders' trade networks in Yiwu and their linkages with African markets. First, I focus on the drivers for the development of Yiwu as a trading hub in general and particularly for African traders in China. Second, I explore the presence of African traders, their composition and their activities in Yiwu. Finally, I discuss African traders' commercial networks in Yiwu and their linkages with African markets.

YIWU: TRADING HUB FOR AFRICAN TRADERS IN CHINA

Following the 1978 economic and industrial reforms in China, entrepreneurship and industrial development have expanded to China's eastern and southern provinces. Growing interests among the Chinese population to set up production bases in those regions correlate with the needs to establish market places. Planning and reforms in the industrial sector facilitated a new entrepreneurial system in China. More and more, enterprises are enjoying increased autonomy but still under strong control of state institutions that determine policies and priority sectors. Such process contributed to industrial production and distribution, leading to flows of commodities based on free market prices that prior to the reforms period were set by the state under guidance planning. One of the major advances that contributed to enhancing China's domestic as well as foreign trade was the development of retail sales. With an improved production capacity, more people were involved in retail business by selling consumer goods. Open entrepreneurial system (more private rather than state-owned businesses), huge production capacity and a more liberal market contributed to creating city-markets in China.

In 1984, as a local government strategy, the development of Yiwu through trade has motivated the city's trade and industry council to create a new market (Lin Yue, 2006). Those changes made Yiwu a world marketplace, and thus Yiwu has risen from a rural area to becoming the world's largest commodities city (Bodomo, 2012). Located in Zhejiang province in eastern China, Yiwu has become an essential business crossroads for the world's traders and entrepreneurs during recent years. Administratively, Yiwu County was upgraded to a county-level City in 1988. Today, the city has caught the eyes of the world, attracting millions of businesspersons from all over the world. Even though it is under the jurisdiction of Jinhua, Yiwu is more known than Jinhua within and outside of China and ranges among the most powerful Chinese cities and counties with a remarkable economic strength (Guo Mu, 2010).

Thanks to comprehensive economic reforms (trade liberalization, private entrepreneurship development and establishment of trade networks and so on) undertaken by Chinese officials, Yiwu is now a "commodities center" in China, providing the world's markets with cheap Chinese consumer goods and sustaining China's economic growth based on exports in the past 30 years. Therefore, Yiwu has been named as the banner of China's market economy. Industrial hubs with factories in Wenzhou, Qiaotou, Datang and other places around Zhejiang province have developed and they supply Yiwu market districts (Lin Yue, 2006).

According to Tim Philipps (2005: 59), "the city of Yiwu functions as a sort of 'Wall Street' for the counterfeiting industry, providing a vast marketplace where hundreds of thousands of counterfeit products are openly traded and 2,000 metric tons of fakes change hands daily." In the Yiwu area, there are, in particular, eight large industrial sectors that have developed: socks, shirts, wool, accessories, zippers, toys, key sticks and printing (Ding, 2007). In addition, the availability of a diverse variety of products is one of Yiwu's main advantages to attract traders. There are 300,000 to 400,000 types of products available in Yiwu (Lin Yue, 2006). Its close location to coastal cities like Hangzhou, Shanghai and Ningbo—the latter hosts the closest port to ship goods from Yiwu—and the development of its transport hub (rail and air transport) to connect to other business cities like Guangzhou, Shenzhen and most recently Hong Kong (from July 2012), drives traders to visit its markets. In these markets, each district is specialised in selling specific products. Therefore more and more foreigners are attracted to engaging in bulk shopping in Yiwu markets for resale in their home countries. During recent years, Yiwu has played an unprecedented role in China's exports which constitute one of the factors of the country's economic growth. The commodities stocked in the "warehouses" in Yiwu are sold to 215 countries and territories of the world (China Customs, 2009). Yiwu is famous for its small commodities' trade and free markets.

The city is known as the "small commodities center" in China with its export markets (国际商贸城/International trade city) ranging from district one to district five in the Futian neighborhood; each of them specialised in distinct commodities. In district 1 there are toys, accessories and handcrafts. In district 2 are hardware, travel items and electronics. In district 3 stationary, sports items and cosmetics are sold. In district 4 there are daily use articles, shoes and socks. District 5 is composed of imported products, bedding and auto-parts.

With Yiwu's export volume in rapid growth and its role in China's broader foreign trade during recent years, China's State Council has favored the establishment of a Customs office in Yiwu in order to enable fast commodity clearance. As the world's largest commodities' market, in October 2002, Yiwu benefited from the opening of a Customs branch under the Jinhua Customs office through the Hangzhou Customs district. In July 2009, a Customs office was opened in Yiwu. Convenient measures were established to speed up the customs' clearance. Before the opening of the Customs office in

Yiwu, the Jinhua Customs office was processing commodities' clearance under its Yiwu branch. According to China Customs (2009), between 2003 and 2008, customs declarations processed at Jinhua Customs office increased from 21,000 to 277,000 and the number of containers rose from 51,000 to 521,000 TEU (Twenty feet Equivalent Unit), thanks to Yiwu's exports. The market districts are strategically located and close to Yiwu's international logistics center which facilitates the transportation of goods to the port of Ningbo and outside of China through Chinese and international shipping companies.

Yiwu has economically grown with the establishment of its markets and the arrivals of foreigners who show interest in doing business there. Their presence has changed the business pattern in the area and with the rest of the world. As the *Times of India* explained, "Yiwu, China's small commodity market in Zhejiang province saw a strong growth in trade with India and fellow BRICS countries in 2011 with the quantum touching US$ 1.03 billion in value terms" (*Times of India,* 20 February 2012). Over time, as trade and business grow in Yiwu, the local government has played an important role in improving infrastructure around the city and connecting it to other places, both domestically and internationally. Beyond finding a wide range of products at competitive prices, the world traders were attracted by the facilities put in place that accompanies their trade activities. The establishment of a Customs office for customs clearance, an international logistics center for the transportation of products to the Port of Ningbo, an international banking system with international money transfer services via Western Union, Money Gram and Postal Money Order, as well as the construction of an international airport which connects to major Chinese and international cities, have all contributed to bringing traders from Africa and around the world to Yiwu. Yiwu goes to great lengths to establish conditions that are supportive of Africans and other foreigners who prove themselves over time to be genuine businesspersons and women (Bodomo, 2012).

Based on local economic policies to create industries, establish markets and build infrastructure in order to facilitate trade both domestically and internationally, the development of trade in Yiwu as a new destination for trade is different from that of Guangzhou, a city known as a traditional trade city in China's domestic and foreign trade history due to its location in the Pearl River Delta and next to Hong Kong. While industries and markets around Guangzhou have developed without economic decisions from the local government, in Yiwu strong interests from the government to build industries, markets and infrastructure have driven business and trade. The policy approach by local officials and entrepreneurs to make Yiwu a trade hub in China's domestic and foreign trade has contributed to accommodating foreign traders, including African traders in Yiwu. Yiwu officials are aimed at building the world's largest "supermarket" for small commodities with supplies to local markets as well as international markets through trade fairs and exhibitions held in the city (Pliez, 2010). Yiwu has been developed purposely by the Chinese authorities as a center for sourcing commodities (Bodomo, 2009b).

With the facilities developed over the years (port of Ningbo, Customs office, Yiwu international logistics center, modern transport systems, international banking systems, etc.), Yiwu remains attractive for African traders who can source a wide range of products in Yiwu markets supplied by factories specializing in specific products and located in Zhejiang province. Within China itself, Yiwu has become a sourcing market for the rest of the country. Such rapid change has been possible through reforms and policies undertaken by local political and economic institutions. Domestic political and economic policies led to Yiwu's transformation to become an important trading hub in China's domestic as well as foreign trade.

Besides the price competitiveness and the variety of products in Yiwu markets, African traders seem more positive about Yiwu's policies and official regulation to accommodate Africans for trade and business compared to Guangzhou. In this regard, in April 2011, an African trade center was opened in Yiwu and almost all African countries have been provided space to set up shops in the 5th district of Yiwu's largest commodities market even though most of the shops are run by Chinese (Cissé, 2012). Furthermore, Yiwu local officials are open to foreigners and invite African traders to trade fairs and exhibitions.[1] City bureaucracies actively facilitate the establishment of foreign businesses in the interest of economic development and social well-being (Marfaing and Thiel, 2014). Due to existing tensions between Africans and Chinese citizens in Guangzhou, (i.e. tensions between traders and police officers and the difficult conditions Africans face in renewing their permits) traders have moved to other Chinese cities, including Yiwu. While in Guangzhou Africans are concentrated in specific areas (mainly Sanyuanli and Xiaobei where they become targets of police controls and assaults), in Yiwu there is no single location where Africans are concentrated to carry out their trade and live. This situation enables them to operate with less difficulty compared to Africans in Guangzhou.

PRESENCE OF AFRICAN TRADERS IN YIWU

Even though the number of African traders in China started growing in the late 1990s and the early 2000s, many Africans, including traders, had already settled in China. Either relocating to China's major trading hubs of Guangzhou or Yiwu from neighboring Asian countries (Thailand, Malaysia, Singapore), the United Arab Emirates following the Asian financial crisis in the late 1990s, their home countries or Europe and the United States, where some of them had established businesses, African traders ventured to China for business opportunities. They first went to Guangzhou and increasingly to Yiwu. In this regard, Guangzhou has been an attractive locale. It is a center of China's domestic and foreign trade due to its location in the Pearl River Delta (which includes manufacturing hubs in neighboring cities such as Dongguan, Shenzhen, Foshan etc.) and its proximity to Hong Kong which is another financial and trade center.

But recently Yiwu has become a trade hub for traders from all over the world, including African traders. Yiwu has developed into an international trade city with the development of a trade center with all the facilities (market districts, logistics center, customs office, etc.). There are over 13,000 merchants from 100 countries and regions residing in Yiwu and dealing with international procurement. Additionally, there are 3,000 foreign enterprises which have set up representative offices in Yiwu and 440,000 foreign traders come and buy every year (Ma Enyu, 2012; Lin Yue, 2006). At Yiwu markets, buyers from Africa and the Middle East constitute the largest numbers among 180 countries represented (Lin Yue, 2006). In 2006, there were 20,311 registered Africans in Yiwu; in 2009 the number increased to 54, 050 and it is still growing (Ma Enyu, 2012). A growing number of African traders are attracted to Yiwu because they can find what they want as well as meet the manufacturers directly, thus eliminating the intermediate links and saving on costs (Ma Enyu, 2012).

While in the past there were African traders travelling to Yiwu to buy "made in China" products to resell in their home countries, most of the African traders who settled in Yiwu arrived in the early 2000s. African traders in Yiwu can be categorized into three groups: the entrepreneurs, the trade agents and the temporary traveling traders (Cissé, 2013). The entrepreneurs have established businesses in Africa, Europe, the United States and Asia. For instance, a Senegalese trader who has been in China for eleven years now, once had businesses in Europe and the United States.[2] The price competitiveness and the wide range of products the Chinese markets offer and the development of Yiwu as an international trade center have driven them to explore business opportunities within and outside China by reaching customers around the world. They had travelled to China before to participate in trade fairs and place orders for businesses set up elsewhere; hence, their awareness of the gradual development and changes which occurred in Yiwu.

African traders in Yiwu take advantage of the market's aggregation function determined by the proximity between production centers and the market districts and the connection between different aspects of trade: manufacturing, communication, sales and logistics. Such developments made them open up registered trading companies which are formally managed by qualified staff in trade, logistics, legal matters, accounting, etc. Many of these traders have become long-term residents of China (often with a one year renewable visa), often with families; quite a few of them have become very wealthy (Pieke, 2012). As well established traders with well settled businesses, they have developed connections with Yiwu officials and are invited to trade fairs and exhibitions and convene at important business events. Yiwu municipal authorities regularly call on the African businesspeople for their opinions (Bodomo, 2012).

However, there are more and more Africans "trade agents" who often operate at the grassroots trade level and seize the trade opportunities China offers. Often with a short-term business or tourist visa, they travel to China to operate on the margins and search for business possibilities. They overstay or travel to neighboring Asian polities (Hong Kong, Macau, Thailand, Malaysia and Philippines) which are visa free destinations for citizens from a number of African countries in order to renew their tourist visas to re-enter China. Most of them are intermediaries and facilitate business between Chinese factories, wholesalers and African traders who travel to Yiwu.

They either run their trading agencies or operate informally by receiving commissions from the Chinese factories' owners, wholesalers and logistics companies' managers. They have established transnational business networks and make use of the new opportunities presented to them through the growing Africa-China economic relations (Müller and Wehrhahn, 2013). With their knowledge of the Chinese markets and business networks they have developed with Chinese sellers, factories and companies, they play an important role in fostering business between African traders who temporarily travel to China and Chinese businessmen. They welcome the African traders who travel to Yiwu, arrange their visits to specific markets or factories to place orders or buy products and organize the logistical procedures for the shipment of products to Africa. They provide different services ranging from accommodation, market tours, warehousing and logistics. Their business relies on trust and long-term relationships with their customers and their Chinese counterparts. Some of them have managed to secure customers from their home countries as well as different African countries.

Even though African traders in this category are operating at the grassroots trade level, they have received a high education and sometimes even earned a university degree.[3] Buying from Chinese factories and wholesalers and reselling in their home countries and other African countries, over time the traders explore other segments of international trade including logistics and money transfers. The money transfer system, even though informal, enables traders to bypass the expensive money transfer costs through formal money transfer companies like Western Union and Money Gram, and travel to their home countries without carrying large sums of money.

Alongside African traders who settled in Yiwu as entrepreneurs and trade agents, more and more Africans regularly travel to China for business purposes. The growing trade relations between African countries and China have encouraged such interests for many African traders to explore the Chinese markets. The African traders in this category are granted a short business visa for a maximum of one month and at times for two to three weeks for their business activities in China. Based on informal connections and trade relations through a family member or friend, they are assisted in China by trade agents. They buy and resell Chinese products in African markets. They either operate as retailers if they own retail businesses or as wholesalers. The products they buy and resell vary from clothing, footwear, hair extensions, and decoration items, and are often sold to low-end consumers. Some of the traders have secured a niche market for high-end products (household appliances, electronics, furniture, etc.) for customers with higher purchasing power.

After Dubai, Hong Kong, Bangkok and Kuala Lumpur, which used to be their favorite destinations in Asia, African traders have discovered the Chinese markets due to trade hubs developed in Guangzhou and Yiwu over time, as well as the establishment of a growing number of Africans in those cities who play a significant role in building trade ties and facilitating business relations between African traders and Chinese businessmen.

AFRICAN TRADERS' NETWORKS IN YIWU AND THEIR LINKAGES WITH AFRICAN MARKETS

Even though established in other regions (Europe, North America and Asia) through African traders' activities in those places, the success of African trade network is based on transnational social and economic networks strongly linked to domestic networks in their home countries. African traders maintain strong ties with fellow traders in their home countries through well-organized trade structures and supply them with products from their host countries. For instance, the Mourides create networks which span several continents linking together their communities in Europe, North America and West Africa as well as maintaining ties with merchants in Dakar (Ebin, 1995).

While in the past African transnational trade networks were based on social ties, in the context of globalization and the interconnectedness of economies, transnational trade networks developed through migration and trade are no longer based on ties between traders of the same country of origin, ethnic group or religion but are rather guided by business activities and economic interactions. While African traders' transnational trade networks are then often based on traders' country of origin, ethnicity or religion (the Yoruba and Igbo from Nigeria and the Mourides from Senegal), more and more the characteristics of businesses determine the African traders' interconnection within and beyond their respective borders. This new form of establishing trade networks drives economic opportunities and contributes to the expansion and diversification of markets.

Trade networks retain important economic functions and shape the possibilities for economic development (Golub and Hansen-Lewis, 2012). In African diaspora trade networks, sharing information and providing mutual information are keys to economic success. Trade networks can also increase the availability of market information essential for trade by helping host-country exporters find buyers and improve their knowledge of the market (Plaza and Ratha, 2011). Transnational trade networks can help manufacturers and wholesalers reach distribution centers based on the relationship they have developed with traders in the same geographical location and beyond; this process facilitates business expansion into new markets. The connection between African traders' host countries, countries of origin and other places where they have business ties is also important to the expansion of trade and trade networks. Besides, the presence of trade networks facilitates all aspects of trading activities; particularly for merchants who travel for a short period of time to specific countries to buy products. Once business collaboration is established through trade networks, the traders settled in overseas markets can provide all services needed (order, purchase, payment and shipment) by itinerant traders who at times do not need to travel abroad for business purposes.

Trade networks in Africa are often based on family networks and long-term business relationships between traders from different places. Long-term relationships facilitate the building of the links among traders (Fafchamps, 2001: 9). In Chinese city-markets, the same situation prevails when African traders deal with their counterparts temporarily traveling to China, Chinese merchants, factories and logistics companies. Most of the time, trust is the only aspect that links traders and businessmen as almost all transactions are informal, based on the characteristics of many African economies' trade environment. But that trust has developed, based on long-term relationships, through family, business, religious or kinship ties. Traders' ties with communities based on a common identity can influence their business relations through trade networks. Often the transactions between African traders in Yiwu and their customers based in Africa do not rely on formal or legal trade systems (for example contract, payment by check, credit, insurance and so on). Businessmen in Africa conduct business transactions with individuals they can trust (Fafchamps et al., 1995). As Fafchamps (2001: 5-6) argues, "Business networks in Africa are shown to play a variety of functions (interlinking, facilitation, and sharing of information about prices and market conditions) and to take many shapes (network affiliation, sharing a common religion or ethnicity and so on)." In Yiwu, the African traders' networks are based on the business relations traders have established regardless of their origins.

For instance, with their already existing networks in Africa and elsewhere, and based on orders placed through the issuance of a letter of credit, African traders in Yiwu supply their customers with products. Well established traders use modern information and communication technologies to advance their commercial transactions, in particular, orders and financial transfers from their customers in Africa and around the world (Tall, 2004). The international information system they have put into place enables them to inquire about their customers' needs and satisfy them (Bertoncello and Bredeloup, 2009). Transactions are based on Incoterm rules (International Commercial Terms) and international trade procedures from the issuance of a letter of credit to the shipment and payment of the order. The connection between business networks and community is therefore important among African traders. McDade and Spring (2005: 17) state, "the new generation of African entrepreneurs are business globalists who organized business enterprise networks consisting of national, regional and pan-African organizations." Social networks predominate in the facilitation of the first international trading trip the traders made (Afolayan, 2011: 8). Albeit competitive, African traders often operate with each other.

In Yiwu, an organization that brings African traders together has been created. The organization brings together traders and entrepreneurs from various African countries. It defends their interests, facilitates their trade and business activities and improves communication with Yiwu local officials and business communities who have already built ties with some well-established African entrepreneurs.[4] Such associations or organizations assist newcomers in their basic needs right after their arrival. In addition, in their trading activities, they are assisted by members of the networks in making contacts with trading partners, providing trade connections and locate factories around Yiwu. African traders' social and business networks are developing in China particularly in Guangzhou and Yiwu where the presence of African traders is becoming more and more important.

Furthermore, as Afolayan (2011:8) argues, "trade networks comprise international trade partners, import and export agencies, friends, self-sponsored relatives/family members, e-commerce, chambers of commerce and lastly masters/mentors." African traders in China help each other to make business connections and they reach out to others for advice and assistance. They spread their economic activities into China and support exports of Chinese consumer goods to mass markets through transnational trade networks between African markets and manufacturing bases and wholesale markets in China (Müller and Wehrhahn, 2013).

Established in China, African traders create multiple connections between African and Chinese markets, businessmen, companies and economies, hence, the transnational business networks. For instance, in order to establish business networks with traders in other African countries, a well-established Senegalese trader in Yiwu has hired other African employees regardless of their country of origin, religion, and ethnicity.[5] African traders in China develop numerous economic relations that cross national state borders and ethnic divisions and thus establish new forms of socio-economic organization that allow a widened perspective on concepts of transnational entrepreneurship (Müller and Wehrhahn, 2013). Established in Yiwu, African traders' networks develop business ties with traders in African markets. Alongside the Chinese traders who set up shops in African countries, more and more African traders who travel or live and own trade businesses in China's city-markets make Chinese goods available in African markets.

One of the author's interviewees at Yiwu international logistics center stated that Africans at the international city of Yiwu constitute 40 percent of the foreign traders.[6] African traders travel to China where they purchase large volumes of a variety of Chinese consumer goods which they resell in their home country and other countries. The goods are often channeled through logistics and shipping companies to reach different urban markets in Africa. In some cases, traders bring back the goods themselves in large trunks and suitcases (Golub and Hansen-Lewis, 2012). Mathews (2011) highlights the way African traders who travel to Hong Kong (Chungking Mansions) bring knock off Chinese products back to their country in their travel bags and suitcases for resale. This is how trade works in China's export markets between foreign traders and the rest world.

With a better knowledge of their home markets and consumers' needs, African traders supply various African markets with "made in China" products. Through Chinese and international logistics and shipping companies in Yiwu, which provide services to different African countries, they ship the products to different African ports via the port of Ningbo. A Chinese logistics company manager mentioned that before the Arab Spring, 30 to 40 containers (40 feet each) a week were sent to Africa through its office.[7] The containers are filled with consumer goods (clothing, footwear, accessories, garments, stationery, furniture, construction material, and so on) purchased at Yiwu market, transported to the port of Ningbo where 98 percent of the products from Yiwu transit before reaching Africa and other continents.[8] While some African traders have the means to acquire and pay for entire containers, others do groupings by buying or sharing cubic meters in a container (Cissé, 2013).

The duration of the shipping depends on the destination country for the containers and the quality of the carrier company. For instance, containers shipped via Evergreen to South Africa from Ningbo reach the port of Durban in 19 days; containers shipped to West, East and Central Africa need 30 days, while those sent to North Africa need 60 days. It is relevant to mention that there is also air freight. But African traders are more involved in the bulk purchase (huge quantity and heavy weight) and usually do not target this mode of transport. The African traders' knowledge of the international logistics chain and its different segments while trading thus makes available a wide range of Chinese products in Africa (Cissé, 2013). Either traveling back and forth from their home countries to China or settled in Yiwu, African traders have expanded their distribution markets for Chinese consumer goods across the continent based on trade networks beyond their national borders.

African traders have secured niche markets in Africa for "made in China" goods. Products shipped to Africa are often sold to wholesalers in different African markets. Those wholesalers supply retail traders who are in the informal trade sector. With the flows of Chinese imports to African countries, many young people, particularly vendors or peddlers, have found business opportunities to support themselves and families (Cissé, 2013). Besides, some of the African traders established in China have their own shops—in their home countries—which are often run by their family members and which they supply with Chinese consumer goods. Like the Chinese shops in Africa, those shops often operate as wholesale as well as retail. Products are not only limited to clothing and footwear but also com-

prise of household equipment, furniture, construction material, etc.,
and target different customers with different purchasing power.

CONCLUSION

Compared to other studies which explored the motivations and sociological aspects of African traders' presence in China, this chapter focused on the African traders' trade networks and their linkages with
African markets through trade and business activities. While China
is the largest source of emigration, today the country has become one
of the most emerging immigration destinations. China's city markets (Guangzhou and Yiwu) have attracted traders and entrepreneurs
from all over. Among those traders are the African traders who in the
past were established in other Asian, European and North American
countries and cities for business purpose. The 1997 Asian financial crisis and the high cost of doing business in Europe and North
America alongside tight immigration policies have driven African
traders to China. Around the beginning of the 2000s, African traders
have also taken the opportunity to migrate to mainland China for
business opportunities.

While some came from other regions of the world, others directly
come from their home countries and settle in China. Guangzhou is
the major destination for most of those African traders due to its
location and its closeness to the "world factories" which supply the
world markets with "made in China" products. But in eastern China today, Yiwu is the world's largest commodities market—within
China's largest export market—and is slowly surpassing Guangzhou
in terms of the African presence. Even though established in China,
African traders have developed strong trade and business networks
with other traders in their home countries. Those networks are based
on business ties rather than social, kinship or religious ties as in
the past. More and more, business interests based on the type of
traders connected through business around the world. With their
knowledge of the Chinese markets, factories and relationship with
Chinese factory owners, logistics companies, customs officials and so
on, African traders' networks in China serve as bridges to deepen-
ing trade and business relationship between them, their counterparts

in Africa and Chinese entrepreneurs. Therefore, they create multiple connections between African and Chinese markets, businesses, companies and economies through their transnational business networks.

REFERENCES

Afolayan, A.A. (2011) 'Dynamics of Mobility of International Traders in Nigeria: Economic Crisis, Globalisation and Visa Situation', paper presented at the IV International Symposium International Network on Migration and Development (INMD) on "Global Crisis and Migratory Strategies: Redefining Migration Policies," May 18, 19 and 20, 2011; at Facultad Latinoamericana de Ciencias Sociales—FLASCO Ecuador Campus. Quito, Ecuador.

Bertoncello, B. and Bredeloup, S. (2009) 'Chine-Afrique ou la valse des entrepreneurs-migrants', *Revue Européenne des Migrations Internationales*, Vol.25, pp. 45-70.

Bodomo, A. (2012) *Africans in China: a sociocultural study and its implications for Africa-China relations*. Amherst/New York: Cambria Press.

Bodomo, A. (2009b) 'The African presence in contemporary China', *The China Monitor*, Issue 36, pp. 4-6. Available at: http://www.ccs.org.za/wpcontent/uploads/2009/04/china_monitor_issue_36_january_2009.pdf [accessed 15 August 2014]

China Customs (2009) 'Yiwu Customs House Opens', available at: http://english.customs.gov.cn/publish/portal191/tab47809/info182737.htm [accessed 19 June 2012].

Cissé, D. (2013) 'South-South migration and Sino-African small traders: a comparative study of Chinese in Senegal and Africans in China', *African Review of Economics and Finance*, Vol.5, No. 1, pp. 21-35.

Cissé, D. (2012) 'The African trade center in Yiwu—is it really for Africans?', Center for Chinese Studies commentary, 18 June. Available at: http://www.ccs.org.za/wpcontent/uploads/2012/06/DC-Yiwu.pdf [accessed 11 August 2014].

Ding, Ke (2007) 'Domestic market-based industrial cluster development in modern China', IDE- JETRO Discussion paper number 88.

Ebin, V. (1995) 'International networks of a trading diaspora: the Mourides of Senegal abroad', In Antoine, P. and Diop, A.B. (eds.) *La ville à guichets fermés? : Itinéraires, réseaux et insertion urbaine*. Dakar: IFAN/ORSTOM.

Fafchamps, M. (2001) 'The role of business networks in market development in Sub-Saharan Africa', In Aoki, M. and Hayami, Y. (eds.) *Community and market in Economic development*, Oxford: Oxford University Press.

Fafchamps, M., Pender, J., and Robinson, E. (1995) 'Enterprise Finance in Zimbabwe', Regional Program for Enterprise Development, Africa Division, The World Bank, Washington, D.C., April 1995.

Golub, S. and Hansen-Lewis, J. (2012) 'Informal trading networks in West Africa: The Mourides of Senegal/The Gambia and the Yoruba of Benin/Nigeria', In N. Benjamin, and Mbaye, A.A. (eds), *The Informal Sector in Francophone Africa: Firm Size, Productivity, and Institutions*. Washington, DC: World Bank.

Guo, Mu (2010) 'The Yiwu Model of China's Exhibition Economy', *Provincial China*, Vol. 2, Issue 1, pp. 91-115.

Lin Yue (2006) 'Le Carrefour du made in China', *Outre-Terre*, No. 15, pp. 187-193.

Ma Enyu (2012) 'Yiwu mode and Sino-African relations', *Journal of Cambridge Studies*, Vol.7, No. 3, pp. 93-108.

Marfaing, L. and Thiel, A. (2014) '"Agents of Translation": West African Entrepreneurs in China as Vectors of Social Change', German Research Foundation Working papers Series N° 4.Available at: http://www.spp1448.de/fileadmin/media/galleries/SPP_Administration/Working_Paper_Series/S PP1448_WP4_Marfaing-Thiel_final.pdf [accessed 11August 2014].

Mathews, G. (2011) *Ghetto at the center of the world: Chungking mansions, Hong Kong*, Chicago: University of Chicago Press.

McDade, B. E. and Spring, A. (2005) 'The 'new generation of African entrepreneurs': networking to change the climate for business and private sector led-development', *Entrepreneurship and Regional Development*, Vol. 17, pp.17-42.

Müller, A. and Wehrhahn, R. (2013) 'Transnational business networks of African intermediaries in China: practices of networking and the role of experiential knowledge', *Journal of Geographical Society of Berlin*, Vol. 144 (1): 82-97.

Pieke, F.N. (2012) 'Immigrant China', *Modern China*, Vol.38, Issue 1, pp. 40-77.

Plaza, S. and Ratha, D. (2011) 'Harnessing Diaspora Resources for Africa', In Plaza, S. and Ratha, D. (eds.) *Diaspora for development in Africa*, Washington, DC: World Bank.

Pliez, O. (2010) 'Toutes les routes de la soie mènent à Yiwu (Chine): Entrepreneurs et migrants musulmans dans un comptoir économique chinois', *l'Espace Géographique*, Vol.39, N°2, pp. 132-145.

Tall, S. M. (2004) 'Senegalese Émigrés: New Information and Communication Technologies', *Review of African Political Economy*, Vol.31, Issue 99, pp.31-48.

The Times of India (2012) 'Yiwu's trade with BRICS countries goes touches $1.03 billion', February 20, 2012. Available at: http://articles.economictimes.indiatimes.com/2012-02-20/news/ 31079598_1_brics-countries-yiwu-indian-businessmen, [accessed 30 July 2012]

Tim, P. (2005) *Knockoff: the deadly trade in counterfeit goods: the true story of the world's fastest growing crime wave*, London: Kogan Page.

NETWORKS, SPHERES OF INFLUENCE AND THE MEDIATION OF OPPORTUNITY: WEST AFRICAN TRADE AGENTS IN CHINA

LAURENCE MARFAING AND ALENA THIEL

INTRODUCTION

Drawing on theories of networked socio-economic life in West Africa, we advance that the types of Ghanaian and Senegalese communities' social organization in Yiwu, Guangzhou and Hong Kong have important effects on their members' entrepreneurial success and upward social mobility. We argue that as an expression of "vernacular cosmopolitanism" (Appiah 1998; Diouf 2000), the circulation of capitals—for example, between established entrepreneurs and newcomers—is controlled by distinct yet mutually integrated networks. While "networks of accumulation" (Meagher 2006, 2010) give preferential treatment to kin- and community-mediated relations, "networks of survival" lack such strong expressions of solidarity. Here, structural factors external to communal life may allow a newcomer to advance in the career and eventually penetrate into a "network of accumulation," in which insights and experiences but also functional contacts with the Chinese business and bureaucratic channels are concentrated. In their capacity to mobilize the spheres of influence, they reach into—be it for members of their network or sporadically the compatriot in urgent need—"networks of accumulation" of

Ghanaian and Senegalese agents in China overlap decisively with the process of community formation.

West African communities in China are constituted of diverse actors including students, diplomats, and artists and, of course, entrepreneurs in various business areas. The scope of this chapter is on those residents who render trade-related services to their predominantly West African clients who come to China for sourcing goods, materials and machines for their businesses back home. Despite this focus on a particular group of economic actors, we advance that classifications of African residents in China that are solely based on their economic activities conceal the internal differentiation of this highly heterogeneous group.[1] By comparing Ghanaian and Senegalese agents in the cities of Yiwu, Guangzhou and Hong Kong, we realized that the emic significations of social positioning, especially within the national communities, and legal status in the Chinese administrative apparatus is just as important as the structural determinants of our informants' businesses (Marfaing and Thiel, 2014). In the present chapter, we look at the effects of these differentiations on solidarity and withdrawal within the Ghanaian and Senegalese communities in China. In particular, we are interested in how transposed local structures are maintained in China, allowing agents to retain normative reference points, while at the same time opening up to bridge into Chinese society. How do these structures—which to varying degrees and capacities enable Ghanaian and Senegalese trade agents in China to mobilize their social and economic networks in order to realize their aspirations—foster agents' economic success, forms of co-operation, and ultimately, community formation in China?

We advance that the analysis of networks is key to answer these questions. Following Granovetter (1973), we argue that the interaction between social and economic life is fundamental to the understanding of African resident entrepreneurs' economic engagement in China. Two forms of embeddedness structure their economic interactions: personal relationships influence actions as a consequence of "relational embeddedness," while "structural embeddedness" refers to the influence of the larger network to which the actor belongs

(Granovetter 1985, 2000). Drawing from her study of Nigerian professional networks, Kate Meagher (2006, 2010) elaborates on this definition of economic networks in West Africa by differentiating between "networks of accumulation," in which resources circulate between more advantaged members, and the "narrower, more poorly resourced personal networks... of survival" (ibid.: 569, 571).[2]

As we will illustrate in the sections presenting our empirical material, we define networks of survival as composed of resource-poor newcomers to China. Lacking the necessary infrastructures and networks of clients as well as Chinese contacts to provide the full array of export related services, the members of these networks usually operate as coaxers. Connectivity and assistance among them is limited and resources flow, if at all, vertically, linking them to the communities' networks of accumulation in which members extend their assistance in cases of emergency—making sure to stress the charitable character of these transactions and thereby maintaining distinct power relations.

Ghanaian and Senegalese networks of accumulation in China, in contrast, are made up of agents who possess considerable capital—be it in the form of financial means, market knowledge, client pools, and probably most importantly, insights and connections into the workings of the Chinese bureaucracy. Able to navigate the system to their advantage, much more than actors in the "networks of survival" at least, these typically full agents (providing all export related services in-house) maintain exclusive boundaries within which these capitals circulate for members' mutual advantage, for example, in the form of assistance with one of the network's newcomers' immigration documentation or the pooling of business information.

Interactions between the two types of networks are characterized by "weak" ties, whereas "strong" ties refer to the relatively exclusive cooperation within a network (Granovetter, 1985). Following on from Granovetter's argument that weak ties provide important links between networks and therefore enable innovation and expansion, not least helping to correct imperfections in transnational business (Broadman, 2007: 22), we argue here that Meagher's classification of networks should not be seen as too static or exclusive. Instead of uncritically adopting the predominant perception of the parallel co-existence of the two kinds of networks, our field data reveal how these network types are consecutive, and with time may flow into each other.

In the following sections, we analyze our ethnographic data collected in three Chinese locations during six weeks of fieldwork in June and July 2013. We are basing our analysis on additional data from repeated fieldtrips to Ghana and Senegal that have been conducted in the period of 2011 to 2014. We start by presenting our methods and field sites, before differentiating the activities and social positions of Ghanaian and Senegalese trade agents in China in terms of their adherence to networks of survival and accumulation. We move on to illustrate the social and economic entanglements of these actors' international business networks and the process of community formation in China. Finally, we trace the links of these networks into Chinese spheres of influence in both economy and administration.

MATERIALS: METHODS AND FIELD SITES

Conducting fieldwork with African communities in China comes with a number of particularities. African communities, especially in Guangzhou, are concentrated in distinct areas. The number of studies carried out on these areas has seen the field extensively researched over the years and many potential informants are taken aback by the ongoing academic interest. Another problem arises from the ambiguous legal status of many African residents in China and the added exposure when talking to other non-African foreigners. We addressed this by following up on the contacts of our informants from Ghana and Senegal, on the one hand, and approaching representatives of the national African communities in China itself, on the other hand, and thereby were able to recruit a total of 76 informants. This strategy allowed us to move from node to node upon recommendation and eventually to negotiate access to the higher echelons of the Ghanaian and Senegalese business networks. Likewise, following network connections led us smoothly from Yiwu to Guangzhou and eventually to Hong Kong as most informants' businesses operated branches in more than one location. Furthermore, this "snowballing" technique not only helped us to get more comprehensive insights into individual enterprises by following up on the employees, partners, colleagues and acquaintances of each informant, but also revealed additional information about the Ghanaian and Senegalese communities' composition and relations of power, seniority but also solidarity. This gave us insights into the networked social organization of Ghanaian and Senegalese business life in China that we argue is fundamental to the process of community formation and the reproduction of this particular sociality in this place.

Hong Kong is the oldest amongst the Chinese sourcing destinations for our informants (Bertoncello and Bredeloup, 2007), having replaced earlier locations like Dubai or Bangkok in the 1990s (Darkwah, 2007; Lavergne, 2002). Still, this former British colony provided us with the smallest corpus of interviews as many entrepreneurs have since returned home or have left for more lucrative locations on the Chinese mainland—especially Yiwu and Guangzhou—only keeping their business addresses in Hong Kong to process financial transactions or receive the occasional African visitor who needs a visa for a neighboring Asian country. For the Ghanaian sample, the city's comparative advantage vis-à-vis mainland China has dwindled since the introduction of visas. As one trader pointed out, his business went from consisting of 99 percent wholesale to 99 percent retail among those 1,000 or so Africans still residing in Hong Kong.[3] In this light, only one Ghanaian and no Senegalese shipping agent could still be recruited for our interviews. This is in line with Le Bail (2009) who counted only about 10 African agencies remaining in Hong Kong.

Guangzhou is a modern city of about 8.2 million inhabitants[4]—though the agglomeration of cities in the Pearl River Delta and the increasing trend of urbanization in Guangdong produce an estimate as high as 14 million.[5] While the city has been receiving foreign business for centuries, the Canton Fair in particular has been attracting foreign entrepreneurs since 1957. The traders in our sample, especially those from Senegal, started to frequent the exhibition

around the late 1970s. Guangzhou is also the city where the presence
of Africans has been most thoroughly studied. Bodomo (2010) states
that very few Africans resided in Guangzhou at the end of 2010,
compared to those Africans travelling to the city as entrepreneurs. In
a context where official numbers are unavailable, the estimates of the
number of Africans living in Guangzhou—tacitly separated into the
francophone quarter Xiaobei and the Anglophone quarter Sanyuanli—vary greatly between 1,000 of the 15,000 foreign residents in
2007 (Bertoncello, Bredeloup and Pliez, 2009; Le Bail, 2009) to
20,000 documented African migrants alone (Haugen, 2012). Some
non-academic sources even quote numbers as high as 100,000.[6] Initially, African migrants consisted mainly of Nigerians and Malians,
though Ghanaians and Senegalese quickly followed (Martinez, 2008;
Le Bail, 2009; Bodomo, 2010). The relevance of this group is acknowledged by the fact that Guangzhou constitutes the headquarters
of the Ghanaian association in China, which encourages all Ghanaians staying in China for more than a few weeks to register
with them.

The influx of African traders into Guangzhou peaked around
2007 to 2008—possibly due to adverse effects of the world financial
crisis on transnational trade but definitely due to the rise of alternative sourcing destinations in countries like Turkey, Vietnam or
Brazil. Since then, our informants claim, living conditions and visa
regulations have also become more restrictive exacerbating both the
economic and social conditions of their stay in China. In fact, while
the legal regulations for residence permits have changed very little
during recent years, our informants have experienced a withering of
bureaucrats' goodwill. At the same time, commercial competition
with Chinese agents continues to grow steadily.

Yiwu, the youngest sourcing destination for informants in our
sample, is a city of 2 million inhabitants in China's Zhejiang
province. In the early 1980s, a government program to establish the
local production of light commodities in this province saw Yiwu
launch the "Developing the city through commerce" campaign. In
1982, Yiwu's municipal government set up the Chouchengzhen
Small Commodity Market (Liu Liqin, 2007: 2). Then, in 1995, the

Yiwu Small Commodity Exhibition began (Luo Xiaojun, 2005: 65). By 2002, five generations of markets had been built in Yiwu, the newest addition to the earlier generations being the Yiwu International Commercial Market. The opening of this megamall supplemented the city's older market complexes with a retail area of 7,000 m², spanning five four-storey pavilions where each section specializes in a particular product. In the mall's tens of thousands of shops, producers display samples of their product range to the 170,000 visitors, among them 2,000 foreign visitors, every day. Despite these dimensions, given the ease of navigating in Yiwu, the resident African population in Yiwu is small. In contrast to Guangzhou, there is no real African quarter or tightly-knit community. Those who have settled in Yiwu are not concentrated in a particular area, though larger numbers can be found in the modern buildings close to the trade center and near the Muslim quarter of Meidah.[7] Nonetheless, both francophone and Anglophone African agents in Yiwu participate in a common business association, meeting more or less regularly to protect their interests in the market against Chinese competition.[8]

AFRICANS IN CHINA: A HETEROGENEOUS GROUP

Regardless of their level of consolidation in China, the main role of agents is to serve as a link between African traders and Chinese producers—typically in the form of dealing with showroom staff and other factory representatives, but also in direct contact with the factories. However, agents differ in their capacity to provide these services. In the course of their careers, they move through a number of social and economic positions in the business and the community. This observation makes Meagher's differentiation between networks of survival and accumulation useful for our purposes given that agents' ability to integrate into and benefit from networks of accumulation, or their exclusion from these, defines their career trajectories in China to a large extent.

Networks of survival

Many informants in our sample arrive in China with virtually no contacts. Instead, they hold various misconceptions about the country's living and working conditions. Given this, they encounter severe difficulties in realizing the entrepreneurial plans that they had projected onto their sojourn to China. Yet, especially those who arrived in the heydays of the Africa-China trade prior to the peak years of 2007/2008 managed to transition from their initial objectives to start a trade business into providing trade-related services instead. Finding themselves in a situation with few legal and economic options besides offering their services as guides, these typically young men start to linger in the lounges of hotels popular among their compatriots and in the areas known for trade with Africans (e.g., Xiaobei or Sanyuanli in Guangzhou). As independent guides, called *coaxers*, they also use their connections in Ghana or Senegal to recruit clients. Sometimes, in cooperation with a travel or clearing agent back home, they receive newcomers in the Chinese market and thereby hope to build their client base. These coaxers provide services such as accompanying clients to markets, identifying suitable suppliers, translating in business deals and negotiating prices. Without their own warehouses or contacts to the shipping companies, however, they either limit their services to these areas, or at some point, build relationships with more established agents in order to make use of the latter's infrastructures with regard to warehousing and loading goods for export. As they predominantly attract small-scale importers who do not possess the means to fill complete containers, these coaxers regularly need to cooperate with other agents in order to make grouped shipments viable.[9] Finally, economic activities are not limited to the procurement of goods but coaxers also incur profits from providing a series of other services. These range from renting out private accommodation to selected customers to catering, laundry and/or hairdressing.

Many coaxers depend on study visas to remain in China legally. While some are genuinely pursuing a degree at a Chinese institution, a large number have simply enrolled in a Chinese language school to secure their immigration documents. The remaining coaxers normally only have temporary business visas, which expire after one month. In order to renew their visas, they have to leave China and reapply. Typically, they do this in Macao due to its proximity to the city of Guangzhou and its practice to process visas upon arrival. Others incur considerable costs to have their visas arranged by agents in Chinese provinces less affected by foreign immigration. However, these temporary solutions do not permit the visa holder to work in China.

With their semi-legal status and the average pay of 300 RMB (*renminbi* or Chinese currency) per day for an independent guide, coaxers quickly come to depend on assistance from their compatriots. However, despite these difficulties, the community associations do not support newcomers' presence in China beyond the dissemination of knowledge about legal regulations and procedures. Carefully managing their reputation with Chinese authorities and future clients, the organized communities prefer to use association members' monthly fees to send a "stranded" compatriot home, paying for the airfare and the penalty for overstaying his or her visa. Similarly, religious associations like the *dahiras* limit their support of newcomers. "There is mutual assistance and we do not drop anyone, but we are here to work. [...] They can sleep at the *dahira* for a maximum of 6 or 10 months, get food sometimes, but it is not self-evident to find a way in this country, there is only business and no jobs for foreigners; and if you do not know anyone here there is no more work in the business either."[10]

Networks of accumulation

In contrast to this narrow notion of solidarity at play within networks of survival, networks of accumulation highlight much closer cooperation. These networks are constituted predominantly of full agents who are autonomous entrepreneurs, not only in the sense that they do not depend on others for the allocation of clients, but also in that they provide all export-related services "in house." Other than their counterparts in the networks of survival, these agents thus provide a wider array of services to their clients who not least often move larger volumes of goods than those clients received by coaxers. For example, they have established trust relationships that allow clients to hire agents for procuring goods on their behalf. With their clients' larger capital volumes and their direct interaction with producers, they also need to verify production sites' capacities and professional standards frequently. Full agents further rent their own warehouses, and in some cases, temporarily stock small amounts of goods in their modern offices. After gathering and checking the various goods, the vast majority of African agents contact a Chinese shipping agent to order a container (few also have their own quotas with the shipping companies), process the export documentation and dispatch the goods to Africa. If their capital base permits, agents secure their clients' loans with Chinese factories who usually agree to deliver up to twice as many goods as paid for if the unpaid portion is guaranteed. Eventually, established agents provide professional services in the realm of market research and consulting across the entire African and Asian sub-regions.

Many of these established agents came with experiences in international trade. Having followed the sequence of their compatriots' popular sourcing destinations over the last two to three decades, their previous destinations included Europe, the United States, Dubai and other Asian destinations like Bangkok and Hong Kong, before they established branches of their businesses in mainland China. In contrast to these truly international businessmen and women, others arrived as coaxers and were lucky enough to come to China at the high point of the China-Africa trade—usually between 2002 and 2005. During these days of the China trade, many of the newcomers were "adopted" and trained by experienced entrepreneurs who taught them the rules of the freight forwarding business and in return reduced their own workload.

Today, this new "generation" of established agents has different motivations to help newcomers gain an economic and social foothold in China (Müller, 2011; Bredeloup, 2012) and frames the practice to train newcomers in the lucrative business of freight forwarding in terms of solidarity. As one Senegalese agent put it, "I employ two Senegalese full-time and some youth just along the line. I am doing it out of solidarity, because I was also taught by someone;

but their chance lasts only six months."[11] In other cases, supporting a newcomer in difficulty is seen as a way to train a suitable assistant or even successor. In all its forms, this activity is a function of the reproduction of the network of accumulation in that such arrangements are always mediated by established relationships and work to reaffirm the network's codes of sociability (Elias, 1987), in particular, the moral obligation to help others to advance in life.

More importantly than the passing on of skills and training, actors in these networks of accumulation organize the circulation of diverse capitals that range from assistance in monetary terms to the sharing of key business information (locations, prices and styles) within exclusive groups. These collaborations function to their mutual benefit. In a similar vein, full agents claim to possess particular "influence" in China by maintaining strategic contacts with the local administration. These contacts are mobilized to help family and friends to acquire residence permits or to mediate in the case of difficulties with the authorities. One informant illustrated this by explaining how he himself submits the visa applications of those close to him, thereby greatly facilitating the application process. Another pointed out how—as representatives of the nationality-based community—the "network of accumulation" needs to maintain good relations with the immigration officials in order to negotiate offenders' release and ultimately repatriation.

In the subsequent sections, we expand on the argument that the roles and positions of full agents as established businesspersons and women and as elders of the nationality-based communities in China overlap to a great extent, thereby playing a fundamental role in the formation of these communities. By presenting two Ghanaian and Senegalese case studies of the social organization of activities and the transfers of capital within networks of accumulation, we analyze in greater detail how these networks reach into spheres of life that extent well beyond—though they are never entirely dissociated from—business. Drawing on the concept of "vernacular cosmopolitanism," we show how networked forms and ideas of ordering communal life are transposed from Ghana and Senegal into China, with the effect of reproducing certain degrees of exclusion towards the inside while opening up towards external, Chinese environments.

WEST AFRICAN ACCUMULATION NETWORKS IN CHINA: SOCIO-ECONOMIC PRACTICES AND COMMUNAL LIFE

In general, the Senegalese enterprises in our sample are in the hands of small groups of relatives in their 40s and 50s. The branches of their typically family enterprises in our three field sites represent a true generational shift. In contrast to the companies' elder generations of traders who possess substantial international business and migration experience in diverse locations across West Africa, Europe and the USA but have learned their trade in the market rather than in formal business schools, these men in their best age possess university degrees from reputable international universities. Following their business establishment in Dubai, they currently operate not only in China but have set up branches in several other Asian countries like Malaysia, Indonesia and Thailand.

Yet, although these companies' kinship-based network of branches expands across several continents and is truly global in its operation, Senegalese agents maintain a distinct "vernacular cosmopolitanism" in their transnational entrepreneurial vision (Appiah, 1998; Diouf, 2000; Rosanders, 2005; Werbner, 2006). To begin with, there is the constant reference point in the original enterprise in the market of Dakar whose founder remains the key—if only symbolic—authority of the company. In view of this, decision making among the transnational branches—facilitated by regular Skype conversations—regarding, for example, further expansion or the allocation of profits is deeply informed by principles of seniority. Most importantly, differences in formal education notwithstanding, these family enterprises continue to operate in the classic structure of recruiting newcomers exclusively within the family network, thus transmitting business skills and circulating capitals along intergenerational "strong ties." The youngest of the family are integrated into the local Senegalese business from an early age onwards before receiving academic training in international universities in Europe, Morocco, the United States and more recently, in China. They are then sent to learn the trade in the Chinese branch of the multinational company, until they receive increasing responsibilities and eventually get to manage their own branch of the company established in the course of further geographical expansion.

In contrast to this common though by no means universal logic of Senegalese business organization, the established agents in our Ghanaian sample to a large extent come from less privileged backgrounds and, by mobilizing "weak ties," have managed to access the network of accumulation in China over the course of the last 5 to 10 years merely by means of gradual accumulation of capital. Hence, they typically arrived in the hey-days of the China trade, either as students or as "hustlers" who, following popular advice, turned to Guangzhou and were lucky to be introduced to a previously established agent who needed assistance with his quickly growing client base. Within few months, they would learn the practicalities of the trade and eventually take "their" clients with them to become independent. Thanks to the business' boom at the time, they quickly established respectable companies active in various areas of investment and often including tight co-operations with Chinese partners.

These Ghanaian agents form the core group of the Ghanaian community association in China. Asked about the criteria of inclusion and exclusion in their group, these actors denied that it had to do with a particular personal wealth, but instead emphasized their experience in the business, which allowed them to pool business information to their mutual advantage, besides what they called their "influence" in Chinese administrative affairs, a point that we will return to in the subsequent section. Through introduction within the community rather than kinship-based mediation, this group occasionally admits individual newcomers—only in one case known to us an agent also brought a relative for training—to receive assistance from an established agent and ultimately inclusion in the network of accumulation. The case of the present community chairman and his former "trainee," the community's secretary, is the pertinent example here.

Though entirely different in their method of inclusion, Ghanaian and Senegalese full agents' activities—though always business oriented—are never solely economic in character but simultaneously situate these actors in complex webs of power relations. A brief look at the literature about the intersection of leadership and economic success underscores this point. Clark's (1997) description of Ghanaian market leaders characterizes the latter as usually the more affluent individuals, capable to spare "unproductive" resources while at the same time gaining substantial status from taking up responsibility for others—a form of subjectivity also described by Werbner (2009) for Botswana elites. For the case of Senegal, Sarr (1999) as well as Marfaing and Sow (1999), and for Niger, Grégoire and Labazée (1993) underscore this point. These leadership positions in the market and society as a whole are reproduced by controlling the flow of resources both horizontally—within the network of accumulation in the form of cooperation but also the obligation to redistribute capitals to newcomers—and vertically, that is, into the networks of survival in the form of charitable assistance in return for gains in status. In view of this, we argue, it is no coincidence that the positions of full agents who are connected within networks of accumulation overlap decisively with those of community leaders. Networks of accumulation, in this light, impinge on the process of community formation in that they provide the central figures in the nationality-based and business associations of Ghanaians and Senegalese in Yiwu, Guangzhou and Hong Kong, which are established to represent and help compatriots in need. The Guangzhou based headquarters of the Ghanaian community in China is staffed with the members of the most successful agents residing there. Successful agents not only represent the main actors of the executive board but also enjoy a particular social status within the Ghanaian community in the city at large, tensions about the skewed representation of genders notwithstanding.[12]

THE DIVERSIFICATION OF NETWORKS: REACHING OUT INTO CHINESE SOCIETY

At the same time, in order to remain open to new opportunities, networks of accumulation do not merely reproduce a West African vernacular cosmopolitanism in China but simultaneously build bridges into wider spheres of influence. They thus do not mobilize their so-cial capital exclusively among themselves but actively reach into the spheres of power in both the Senegalese or Ghanaian state respec-tively, and the local Chinese bureaucratic and business realms.

Working with Chinese administration

As has been referred to already, successful West African trade agents in China, who are also at the center of the nationality-based as-sociations, often mobilize their contacts to relevant players in the Chinese system to assist compatriots in acute need. However, their knowledge of the relevant channels of the Chinese administration also turns them into invaluable mediators and consultants in larger African-Chinese relations. To return to our case studies quoted above, established Senegalese entrepreneurs in China play a distinct role in advising Senegalese officials on business and diplomatic af-fairs, including large state sponsored projects, to be implemented in Senegal. The visit of the Senegalese President to China in February 2014 included a Senegalese businessperson from Yiwu in the dele-gation. In China, the influence of these entrepreneurs allows them to facilitate visa applications for their close kinship network and the smoothing of administrative and legal hurdles for their relatives. Though they limit these services to members of their family, their status and reputation in the business besides their substantial knowl-edge of Chinese social, economic and administrative ways of doing has made this family unofficial spokespersons of their countrymen in China. In the city of Yiwu, the Municipal Justice Bureau concerned dealing with foreigners in legal difficulty has three non-Chinese vol-unteer mediators, one of whom is a Senegalese.[13]

Such "influence"—as difficult as it is to confirm our West African informants' statements from the point of view of their Chinese counterparts—may not least take the form of being recruited for diplomatic purposes in case the embassy in Beijing is too far away or relatively unconcerned with trade-related issues concentrating in Guangzhou, Hong Kong or Yiwu. The group of Ghanaian agents that represent the leadership of the "Ghanaian community in Chi-na"—that is the nationality-based association of all Ghanaian residents in the country—claims to be well connected to the immigration officials in the city in their capacity as mediators in case a compatriot is facing prosecution. While such connections are little surprising given the association's *raison d'être* to assist countrymen in difficulty, what was more striking was the Chinese government's choice to approach this body rather than the Ghanaian embassy in Beijing when in June 2013, a large number of Chinese nationals was arrested in Ghana with charges of illegal mining (*galamsey*).

However, political influence is not the only sphere of influence that Ghanaian and Senegalese networks of accumulation in China are arguably entering. According to Kate Meagher (2006: 553f), "social networks [...] engender trust and flexibility, reduce transaction costs, and facilitate integration into the global economy." Especially, "inter-firm organizational networks" that are constituted by "subcontracting and informal borrowing, based on a combination of proximity, social ties, and considerations of cost and skill" may play this role (ibid.: 561f). In the following, we therefore explain how Ghanaian and Senegalese full agents expand their networks into the realms of the Chinese economy beyond mere customer relationships.

African business networks with Chinese participation

A small and doubtlessly only the most successful group of our informants diversified their forwarding businesses into what they presented as African-Chinese "joint ventures." Though the concrete form of these partnerships remained unclear, the associated activities factually relied on both parties' joint capital (production sites, labor and machinery) and risk taking. Asked about the nature of his cooperation with a Chinese partner, one Senegalese informant responded, "you can call this whatever you want, I own the majority of the shares, I produce, I pay my 250 workers and I sell."[14] Another Ghanaian explained about his partnership that it is "49 percent only on paper, in reality it is 50-50."[15] This same informant clarified the advantage of forming a joint venture with a Chinese partner, especially in the informal spheres of doing business. In his words, the Chinese partner signs all deals in order to discourage suppliers from cheating them. The partner's tacit knowledge of Chinese bureaucracy is equally acknowledged as a major asset.

Another form of extending business networks into Chinese society is by engaging in subcontracting and privileged partnerships. Here, African entrepreneurs source out some of their clients to partnered Chinese businesses, which eventually can lead to trusted and longer-term relationships, which usually enforce professional standards and are a source of innovation for the parties involved.[16] This may take the advanced form of cooperation where the objective is to transfer their business to Africa. Though some of our informants stress the desire to become completely independent of China, many also express the plan to make the move with Chinese partners and Chinese machinery, which they deem more suitable for African needs and conditions. "If a European machine costs 100,000 USD, I can buy five Chinese. Even if one breaks down, I still have four more running."[17] These plans then involve Chinese engineers and instructors, who are sent by the Chinese producer of machinery or materials to enhance the local establishment of the product.

By mobilizing their economic success, their social, familial and sometimes religious connections, besides their intimate knowledge of and importance in the Africa-China trade, big African businesspersons and women in China manage to relate to the Chinese business and administration because of their integration in networks of accumulation. This interlacing of West African networks and Chinese economic and to some extent local political life indicates that networks of accumulation are not mere West African transpositions of ordering socio-economic relations but represent complex adaptations to Chinese realities, opening up to them and integrating them to their advantage.

CONCLUSION

We set out in this chapter to trace the networked social organization of Ghanaian and Senegalese trade agents residing and working in the Chinese cities of Yiwu, Guangzhou and, to a smaller extent, Hong Kong. Adopting Meagher's differentiation between networks of survival as opposed to networks of accumulation, we juxtaposed two sets of economic actors in the African forwarding business in China who differs fundamentally with regard to the services they render and thus their potential for accumulation. We advanced that these agents' opportunities depend largely on the newcomer's integration in the relevant networks and the circulation of capitals within these. In this light, due to their lack of access to networks of accumulation, coaxers have fewer chances to realize their plans in China. In contrast, apprentices of established agents come to be embedded in networks of accumulation, where they learn to exploit the capital and skills that circulate within these realms in order to pursue their strategies of expansion in China.

Typically, this takes the form of young people receiving training from more established agents. In the Senegalese networks in China, despite some exceptions that involve partnerships between peers of an age group of businesspersons, newcomers are often family members: they attend Chinese schools and simultaneously are trained in the enterprise. Ghanaian newcomers, in contrast, tend to access apprenticeships and training predominantly through the mediation of the Ghanaian community association in China.

Nonetheless, although networks of accumulation tend to reproduce themselves with regard to their relatively restrictive selection of newcomers, they do not remain exclusive. Slower and less secure processes of accumulation in the networks of survival with time allow newcomers to move consecutively from one kind of network into the other. In particular, those coaxers who arrived at a time of heightened opportunity—though they initially came with very little social or financial capital—slowly accumulated the resources that allowed them to gain inclusion into the networks of accumulation. In other words, access to networks of accumulation, in addition to the kin-based mechanism of apprenticeships, may be gained by demonstrating success in the business and insider knowledge of the Chinese society.

In addition to this mechanism of inclusion, networks of accumulation make exceptions to their exclusivity by opening themselves towards various spheres of opportunity. In view of this, both Senegalese and Ghanaian agents' strategies in China can be summarized as a maneuvering and overlapping system of religious, familial, entrepreneurial but also political spheres in which capitals such as financial assistance, business information and training circulate. Actors move between these spheres according to their need and without ever leaving their own network by using the network overlaps as gateways. In our view, the actors and relationships within and between various networks of African residents in China can be illustrated in the following model.

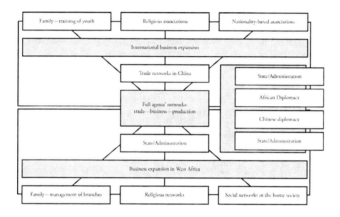

Figure 1: Model of West African trade agents' network ties between Africa and China

We have further illustrated in this chapter how West African trade agents in China mobilize an array of relationships from their different networks in order to ensure their entrepreneurial success. In this light, our model illustrates how the networks of Ghanaian and Senegalese agents in China provide ties with the nationality-based associations in China, mainly by acting as the key representatives of these institutions and by mobilizing their knowledge of and contacts with the Chinese society to assist compatriots in need. Community associations cannot function without these key actors just as the networks of accumulation depend on their nationality-based associations to reproduce themselves and expand their spheres of activity and influence.

Networks of accumulation further create ties with Chinese society, though for methodological reasons less is known about the
mutuality of these relations. From the point of view of our interlocutors, their business success translates into influence, both in
social and political terms, and integrates them to some extent into
the diplomatic relations between different Chinese authorities and
their home societies. Finally, agents' networks of accumulation rely
on a strong connection to their African home societies. Social and
business relationships with the home country act as vehicles for the
transmission of values and modes of behavior into China. Networks
thus represent a delocalization of operating modes from networks
that have their sources in the agents' places of origin. Ultimately,
China is only one stage for the performance of transnational business success which over the course of generations has undergone a
complex expansion of networks through various stages—from the
West African sub-region, Europe and America, Dubai, and Bangkok
to China, and more recently, to new business hubs like Vietnam,
Turkey or Brazil. Along these stations, generations of entrepreneurs
activate and adapt these networks to the respective contexts. Yet, irrespective of location, the validation of the entrepreneurial success
takes place largely also at home. Because of this orientation towards
home, transnational entrepreneurs like the Ghanaian and Senegalese
trade agents in our sample act as conveyors of travelling ideas that
potentially bring about change in the various contexts of their activities (Giese & Marfaing).

In sum, China, because of its rapid economic development in the
export of goods over the last 20 years, acts as a catalyst and emancipatory opportunity for many West African entrepreneurs. Yet, the
key to success lies to at least the same extent in the Ghanaian and
Senegalese mode of operating in social and economic networks. The
processes at play in this interaction of Chinese political and economic conditions for investment and West African entrepreneurs'
vernacular cosmopolitanism in an interconnected world challenge
researchers to rethink some of their categories, for example the much
to quickly applied homogenizing label of African migrants in China.
The movement of our informants between networks valorizes their

status, rendering them fully autonomous and highly experienced entrepreneurs who cannot be subsumed under this category. In addition to this temporal fluidity and porous classifications, we need a more interactive or circular concept of the flow of ideas between Africa and China. Africans in China, according to their social and economic status, act as translators of Chinese ideas and experiences into their places of origin. We have described elsewhere (Marfaing and Thiel, 2014) how these translations reflect at all levels of social and economic life, for example, the sustainable use of public space, the arrangement of homes but also business practices such as work ethics. Yet, Africans are not merely at the receiving end but extend their significations of ordered (networked) social life into their communities in China. These communities in turn embody the future of African-Chinese encounters in their aspiration to return to and produce in Africa.

REFERENCES

Appiah, Kwame Anthony (1998) "Cosmopolitan Patriots." In: Pheng Cheah and Bruce Robbins (eds.), *Cosmopolitics: Thinking and Feeling beyond the Nation.* Minneapolis: University of Minnesota Press, 91-116.

Bertoncello, Brigitte and Sylvie Bredeloup (2007) "De Hong Kong à Guangzhou, de nouveaux 'comptoirs' africains s'organisent." *Perspectives chinoises* 98(1): 98-110. Online since 01 January 2010, accessed September 2013 http://perspectiveschinoises.revues.org/2053

Bertoncello, Brigitte and Sylvie Bredeloup (2009) "Chine-Afrique ou la valse des entrepreneurs-migrants." *Revue européenne des migrations internationales* 25(1):45-70.

Bertoncello, Brigitte, Sylvie Bredeloup, and Olivier Pliez (2009) "Hong Kong, Guangzhou, Yiwu : de nouveaux comptoirs africains en Chine." *Critique internationale* 44:105-121.

Bodomo, Adams (2010) "The African trading Community in Gangzhou: An Emerging Bridge for African-China Relations." *China Quarterly* 20:3 693-707.

Bredeloup, Sylvie (2012) "African Trading Post in Guangzhou: Emergent or Recurrent Commercial Form?" *African Diaspora* 5: 27-50.

Bredeloup, Sylvie (2013) "The figure of the adventurer as an African migrant." *Journal of African Cultural Studies* 25(2): 170-182.

Broadman, Harry G. (2007) *Africa's silk road: China and India's new economic frontier.* Washington: World Bank Publications.

Cissé, Daouda (2013) "South-South migration and trade: African traders in China." Policy Briefing, Center for Chinese studies n°4/2013. Online, accessed November 2013 http://www.ccs.org.za/?cat=64

Clark, Gracia (1997) "MARKET QUEENS. Innovation within Akan Tradition." *Annals of the New York Academy of Sciences* 810: 173–201.

Darkwah, Akosua (2007) "Work as Duty and as Joy. Understanding the role of work in the lives of Ghanaian female traders of global consumer items." In: Sharon Harley (ed.), *Women's labor in the global economy: speaking in multiple voices.* Piscataway: Rutgers University Press, 206-220.

Dittgen, Romain (2010) "L'Afrique en Chine: l'autre face des relations sino-africaines?!" *Economie*, China Institute. Online, accessed September 2013 http://www.china-institute.org/articles/
L_Afrique_en_Chine_l_autre_face_des_relations_sino_africaines.pdf

Diouf, Mamadou (2000) "The Senegalese Murid Trade Diaspora and the Making of a Vernacular Cosmopolitanism." *Public Culture* 12(3): 679-702.

Elias, Norbert (1987) *La société des individus*. Paris: Fayard.

Gaborit, Marie (2007) "Les stratégies d'acteurs chinois et leur rôle dans le développement de la coopération sino-africaine. Les cas du Sénégal et de la Mauritanie", Dissertation at the Institut français de géopolitique, Université Paris VIII.

Giese, Karsten and Marfaing, Laurence (eds), (forthcoming) "Entrepreneurs africains et chinois. Les impacts sociaux d'une rencontre particulière, Paris Karthala.

Granovetter, Mark (1973) "Strength of weak ties." *American Journal of Sociology* 78: 1360-1380.

Granvoetter, Mark (1985) "Economic Action and Social Structure: The Problem of Embeddedness." *American Journal of Sociology* 91: 481-510.

Granovetter, Mark (2000) *Le marché autrement . Les réseaux dans l'économie*. Paris Desclée de Brouwer (Sociologie économique).

Haugen, Heidi Østbø (2012) "Nigerians in China: A Second State of Immobility." *International Migration* 50(2): 65-80.

Lavergne, Marc (2002) "Dubaï ou la métropolisation incomplète d'un pôle en relais de l'économie monde ." *Cahiers de la Méditerranée* 64: 257-296.

Le Bail, Hélène (2009) "Les grandes villes chinoises comme espace d'immigration internationale: le cas des entrepreneurs africains." *Asie Visions* *19*. Online, accessed December 2013 http://www.ifri.org/?page=detail-contribution&id=5570

Liu, Liqin (2008) "Cong 'Jimao Huan Tang' Dao 'Maoyi Quanqiu' (From 'Chicken Feather for Sugar' to 'Trading Globally')." *China Market* 2008 (47): 7-11.

Luo, Xiaojun (2005) "Xiaoshangpin Shichang Shangwu Chengben De 'Langnan Jueze': Yiwu Xiaoshangpin Shichang Shangwu Chengben De Wenjuan Diaocha Yu Fenxi" (The "Dilemma" of Business Costs in a small Commodity Market: A Questionnaire Survey and Analysis on the Business Costs in Yiwu Commodity Market*). Zhejiang Economy* 5: 31-3.

Martinez, Olivier (2008) "Connexions territoriales entre Afrique et Asie: rôle et influence des commerçants malien, répercussions en termes de 'développement local à distance'." *Actualités de la recherche sur les migrations maliennes*, Bamako: FLASH.

Grégoire, Emmanuel and Labazée, Pascal (1993) *Grands commerçants d'Afrique De l'Ouest. Logiques et pratiques d'un groupe d'hommes d'affaires contemporains.* Paris: Karthala.

Marfaing, Laurence and Sow, M. (1999) *Les opérateurs économiques au Sénégal, entre le formel et l'informel (1930-1996).* Paris: Karthala.

Marfaing, Laurence and Thiel, Alena (2014) "Agents of Translation": West African Entrepreneurs in China as Vectors of Social Change, Working Paper of the SPP 1448, No 4, http://www.spp1448.de/fileadmin/media/galleries/SPP_Administration/Working_Paper_Series/SPP1448_WP4_Marfaing-Thiel_final.pdf.

Matthews, Gordon and Yang Yang (2012) "How Africans Pursue Low-End Globalization in Hong Kong and Mainland China." *Journal of Current Chinese Affairs* 41(2): 95-120.

Meagher, Kate (2006) "Social capital, social liabilities, and political capital: Social networks and informal manufacturing in Nigeria." *African Affairs* 105: 553-582.

Meagher, Kate (2010) *Identity economics: social networks & the informal economy in Nigeria.* Suffolk, New York: Boydell & Brewer Ltd.

Müller, Angelo (2011) "New Migration Processes in Contemporary China—The Constitution of African Trader Networks in Guangzhou." *Geographische Zeitschrift* 99(2): 104-122.

Pliez, Olivier (2010) "Toutes les routes de la soie mènent in Yiwu (Chine). Entrepreneurs et migrants musulmans dans un comptoir économique chinois." *Espace Géographique* 2: 132-145.

Rosanders, Eva Evers (2005) "Cosmopolites et Locales: Femmes Sénégalaises en Voyage." *Afrique & Histoire* 2(4): 103-122.

Sarr, Fatou (1999) *L'entrepreneuriat féminin au Sénégal. La transformation des rapports de pouvoirs.* Paris: Harmattan.

Şaul, Mahir and Pelican, Michaela (2014) "Global African Entrepreneurs: A New Research Perspective on Contemporary African Migration." *Urban Anthropology* 43 (1): 1-16.

Werbner, Pnina (2009) "Dialogical subjectivities for hard times: expanding political and ethical imaginaries of subaltern and elite Batswana women." *African Identities* 7 (3): 299-325.

Werbner, Pnina (2006) "Vernacular Cosmopolitanism." *Theory Culture Society* 23: 496-498.

STRUCTURE AND AGENCY: AFRICANA IMMIGRANTS IN CHINA

CARLTON JAMA ADAMS

INTRODUCTION

This chapter addresses some of the challenges faced by Africana immigrants in China from the perspective of structure and agency. By "Africana," I mean peoples from Africa and the worldwide African diaspora. Following a review of the core concepts in the literature, I discuss the structural changes currently evident in China and how these changes affect the sense of agency in domestic migrants and foreign immigrants. This is followed by an overview of the literature of Chinese perceptions of race. That structural framework sets the stage for a discussion of the features of the contemporary Africana population in China followed by an explanation of the methodology used and profiles of the subjects. In the results section, issues of home, reflexivity, structure and agency, relations with the Chinese, enclaves, race and religion and intimacy are discussed. The tentative conclusion is that for Africana immigrants agency is often enhanced by the deployment of their intellectual skills that are in demand in China but is constrained by the exercise of religion and the pursuit of intimacy. Many Africana immigrants therefore experience an enhanced sense of subject well-being in the areas of cognition and material resource acquisition, impact positively on some aspects of Chinese society, even while being constrained by other features of that society.

With its integration into global markets, and its expanding economy, China has firmly embraced modernity concerning its emphasis on knowledge mastery, innovation, and wealth accumulation. This in turn drives an insatiable demand for both local and foreign talent, making China an increasingly attractive destination for new classes of immigrants (Skeldon, 2012). As part of this demand, the Africana population has increased considerably since the 1998 Asian financial crisis and has become more diverse. African immigrants are drawn to China as a site for an enhanced sense of agency in relation to self-development, recognition of talent and the generation of wealth. Immigrants that possess tertiary level intellectual skills and valid visas experience high degrees of mobility and status, and this allows them to garner well-paying work in China. This is in contrast to the experiences of some low-skilled Africana traders who might not have valid visas, experience little mobility and low status, and are always at risk to be exploited and deported (Haugen, 2012).

While self-growth in the areas of knowledge and wealth are abundant in China, extant structural arrangements as manifested in socio-political policies can constrain self-growth in areas such as spirituality and rights advocacy. In addition, Chinese antipathy toward foreigners, alongside the structure of Africana immigrant communities, makes it challenging for both groups to build substantive personal relationships with each other.

Despite the apparent marked increase in the Africana migrant population over the past two decades research that documents issues of subjective well-being and mobility is quite sparse (Bodomo, 2010, 2012; Haugen, 2011, 2012). There is a modest sense of the degree of mobility that informs their exercise of agency. In addition, coming into focus are the features of a host structure that offers cognitive and material opportunities but strictly limits advocacy, discriminates based on race and religion, and is ambivalent and at times hostile toward foreigners and other sources of socio-political difference.

The degree of agency and mobility experienced by the Africana migrant population is diverse. The most mobile are those with highly desirable skill sets, valid visas and an established and legitimate income source. Employees of western and Chinese corporations, credentialed teachers of English with contracts, and traders with valid visas and a thriving export business experience high degrees of agency and mobility (Bodomo, 2012). By contrast, immigrants on expired visas with poor paying jobs or intermittent work tend to experience constrained agency and low degrees of mobility (Haugen, 2012). Some traders, former students and some consultants and teachers of English can be found in this group.

So the degree to which immigrants to China can expand their sense of agency hinges, in part, on possessing a valid visa, being technically qualified, and being curious, reflexive, and creative. A robust sense of agency is also influenced by such structural features as the socio-economic demand for high value products, the balance between the historical antipathy toward foreigners and the contemporary desire for their talent, the ability to curb racist thinking and the degree of mobility permitted to immigrants.

In this chapter, using an interdisciplinary approach, I explore the interaction between the structures in which Africana immigrants are embedded and their capacity to enhance their sense of agency. I introduce the concept of adaptive ambivalence to explain the stance taken by immigrants who have reaped clear cognitive and material benefits from being in China but are also unfulfilled with regards to their communal, spiritual and intimacy needs. I will also discuss the theoretical approaches to structure and agency concerning China in the context of dealing with its own development agenda in a globalized world. This will be followed by a discussion on the opportunities and challenges for Africana immigrants.

LITERATURE REVIEW

Structure, Agency, and Mobility

Increased economic opportunities as a result of changes in the structure of the global economy, alongside an increase in the accessibility, affordability and convenience of air transportation and communications, have fuelled increased levels of migration. The economic nature of much of this migration favors those immigrants who are technically skilled and creative, psychologically resilient, and are embedded in well-resourced support networks. Structure therefore facilitates but can also limit the opportunities for immigrants to work on their varied self-projects.

Structure speaks to a set of schemas or ways of thinking that facilitate or constrain social actions (Sewell, 1992). Traditions, ideologies, policies, and laws all speak to influential schemas that guide social action and are not necessarily conscious (Sewell, 1992). These actions tend to be recurrent, to the degree that entities within the structure can command resources to increase the likelihood of such reproduction. At the same time, a given structure is comprised of relationships between a diverse set of stakeholders with often differing schemas and access to resources (Bakewell, 2010). Some are in comity and others in tension with each other because of competing schemas or differing interpretations of a given schema. Structures therefore do not faithfully and automatically reproduce themselves. Schemas developed for a given context are often used creatively in other contexts, thereby generating unanticipated outcomes and increased space to exercise agency (Sewell, 1992).

Agency can be defined as the degree to which the individual has some authority over his actions and resources (Hitlin & Elder, 2007). Agency extends beyond the physical and psychological assets of the individual and extends to the social. According to Sewell, "Agency entails an ability to coordinate one's actions with others and against others, to form collective projects, to persuade, to coerce, and to monitor the simultaneous effects of one's own and others' activities" (1992: 21). The interpretive room within a given schema makes possible the capacity to generate surprise, difference, and change. Structures are therefore not homogenous, monolithic or immutable and this makes possible the exercise of a form of agency that facilitates the individual acting in concert with others to bring about both personal and social change. Indeed, "Personal agency is, therefore, laden with collectively produced differences of power and implicated in collective struggles and resistances" (Sewell, 1992: 21).

The individual's sense of agency is influenced by multiple factors including the elements of the structure attach to his social markers such as race/ethnicity, nationality, gender, religion, skills profile, immigration status, and organizational affiliations. In addition, the exercise of agency is influenced by how informed the migrant is about such elements and his ability to be reflective and devise strategies, where necessary, to limit constraints and expand his sense of agency. Such reflectivity should include the immigrant having a realistic sense of his strengths and weaknesses and being able to assess objectively whether the given structures within which he is embedded will constrain or facilitate him achieving his desired goals. Whether enacted by individuals or group entities, agency is an inherent feature of structure and a factor in facilitating or constraining other actors within the structure (Sewell, 1992).

Mobility, then, is a function of the quality of the agency that the immigrant can exercise. As a rule, immigrants who possess skills desired by host countries are granted relatively easy access and therefore experience high degrees of mobility with regards to work and recreation. Creative workers, of which some immigrants are a subset, are drawn to structures that appreciate their skill sets and provides them with the resources to be highly productive (Florida, 2002; Strenger, 2013). Shanghai and Guangzhou are such settings in China (Farrer, 2010).

To be sure, there are links between agency, structure and personal development for an emerging and under-studied cohort of Africana immigrants in China.

Immigrants embed in a host structure, they will find some aspects attractive, while other aspects can somewhat constrain the optimal degree of agency necessary to pursue their life projects successfully. Some Africana immigrants with whom I spoke in China speak of the abundant cultural and economic opportunities but others also speak of the sense of being seen as undesirables. This diverse range of perceptions speaks, in part, to larger structural changes in China that have profound implications for ways of thinking about the self in the context of one's sense of agency, regardless of whether one is a citizen or an immigrant.

The first of these changes is the halting but persistent push by China, over the past one hundred years to modernize itself (Hui, 2009; Mitter, 2004). The desire to meet the material demands of its citizens and to be a respected and influential nation on the world stage has resulted in profound changes in how China responds to external factors such as globalization (Hui, 2009). One observes demands for a more open Chinese society that is responsive to worldwide market forces and that should adhere to evolving standards regarding basic human rights and the paramountcy of the rule of law (Fei, 2011). Given these pressures there is an intense interest in technologies and materials originating from the West. The human-scale challenges of modernity, such as human rights, and the constraining of gross wealth inequality receives less attention (Kleinman et al., 2011).

The pursuit of individual agency is gradually challenging the eons-old model of individuality being subordinated to the group whether it is family, emperor, or state. The demands of its economy and the newly deployed sense of individual autonomy have resulted in tremendous internal migration, creating a vast indigenous internal diaspora on China's eastern seaboard (Davin, 1998, 2009; Taylor, 2007). The aspirations of these internal migrants, and the challenges they face, are often similar to those of many of the foreign immigrants of Africana heritage. Chinese internal migrants aspire to achieve higher incomes and greater subjective well-being (Simpson, 2013; Taylor, 2007). They experience high degrees of discrimination, and are often underpaid and have difficulty accessing work permits and social services (Solinger, 1999; Lu & Zhou, 2013). The outcome is often mixed with increased income and a greater knowledge of the world (Davin, 1998), alongside mental health problems (Xiao et al., 2013).

In its quest to be a fully developed modern state, China looks to its citizens and to the West to provide knowledge and skills to facilitate its status as a technological super-power. Many immigrants and migrants therefore find themselves embedded in cultural spaces in considerable ferment where there is little of the stasis and lack of imaginative places typical of their original homes. China faces many structural challenges in its modernization project, three of which stand out. The first is the legacy of the immediate past in terms of the pain associated with the predations of Britain, Germany and

Japan from the late nineteenth to mid-twentieth century (Spence, 1990). Unfair economic treatment, political subordination and the terror and destruction of war still informs how China views the external world. One consequence of this is a periodic heightening of China's longstanding wariness and at times antagonistic stance toward outsiders.

Another consequence of the immediate past is that millions of Chinese citizens bear the psychological scars of the excesses of the "Cultural Revolution era," such as the loss of status or the lack of tertiary-level education alongside many of the younger generations who are also struggling to find their way, given the neoliberal policies introduced by Deng in 1978 (Hui, 2009). These policies introduced neoliberal practices such as unfettered markets, drastic downsizing of the state sector and a concomitant loss of health and housing benefits (Hui, 2009). So the sense of both political and national humiliation, and personal pain as a result of these structural changes, deeply informs how many Chinese go about pursuing their specific life projects.

The second challenge is that while the increased availability of material and improved physical infrastructure in China has been dramatic and relatively quick, the same cannot be said for the structures that address the psychosocial needs of its citizens. This has a resulted in what Fei refers to as an "incomplete modernity" where such features as individual rights, safe consumer products and services and ethical state and corporate actors are less than adequate. Consequently, the individual often lacks the necessary institutional structures to create safe places in which to love and work.

The third challenge is facilitating a sense of community and ethical behavior that manages the tensions between traditional and sometimes archaic rules governing commitment, the newfound sense of autonomy and voluntary altruism, and the neoliberal driven risks of mindless consumption, unethical behavior and alienation. Hope and possibility are keenly felt, however, especially among the millions of residents on China's eastern seaboard, many of whom are internal migrants, mostly from rural communities in China's vast hinterlands (Taylor, 2007). Within this era of rapid change and the less than adequate structures, there are myriad opportunities, albeit not without the aforementioned risks, to explore, cultivate and express many aspects of the self in ways previously unimagined. These opportunities are not all limited to Chinese citizens but are also appealing, and to some degree accessible, to non-Chinese nationals who are open-minded, curious, and psychologically resilient.

So for immigrants there is a sense of being at a time and place in which their desires for adventure and opportunity resonates, however haltingly with the ongoing Chinese project of selectively privileging individual autonomy and creativity (Kleinman et.al., 2011). Therefore, places are created for both internal migrants and foreign immigrants to think of ways to actualize hereto unimaginable or unrealizable self-projects. These initiatives in self-growth result in ongoing challenges to established schemas. The creativity that China needs to harness requires coordinated aspects of structure, an ethical framework to constrain destructive side effects such as an unfettered individualism, rampant corruption, environmental degradation, and the fraying of the social safety net. China must also make accommodation with a recent past in which many were harmed by systemic failures (Kleinman, et al., 2011). There are also pressing demands for a more inclusive stance toward both internal and foreign ethnic diversity.

Chinese Perspectives on Race

Peoples of Africana heritage have been documented as being in China as earlier as the seventh century (Wyatt, 2010). They were groups of traders and others who were enslaved persons (Akyeampong, 2000; Jayasuriya, 2006). From the sixteenth century, because of the trading and colonizing activities of the European powers, one sees more mention of Africana persons in Asia and specifically in China. Dikotter in his detailed history of the attitudes of Chinese elites to race from antiquity to 1950 noted a stance that was part xenophobia and part racism toward non-Chinese peoples (Dikotter, 1992). China long ago established a hierarchy of barbarianism, with Blacks occupying the lowest rung, being furthest removed from the civilized as embodied by the Chinese Han people. Whites were also denigrated but were also feared because of their possession of superior technology.

Blackness was not essentialized as meaning out of Africa or peculiar to those with Black pigment; blackness could also speak to any group perceived as ignorant. Fennell in her overview of Chinese thinking on race notes that the Chinese thirst for knowledge meant that it was not immune to the essentialized racism embedded in the enlightenment thinking of the West that was advocated by Western elites residing in China (Fennell, 2013). Such racialized thinking was inextricably linked to Western scientific classification that the Chinese venerated. Social Darwinism as manifestation of racialist scientific thinking was used to justify the inferior outcomes of subordinated persons of color. This misuse of Darwin was in the context of attempts by Chinese elites to understand what made the Western nations superior. Here Darwin's thinking was misinterpreted to mean that race-based competition would result in the best group succeeding, assuming that such a group was homogeneous and was united in purpose. The Chinese elites made the erroneous assumption that the superiority of the white race had a genetic basis and did not factor in the role of structural racism in contributing to the inferior performance of subordinate groups. Fennell also notes that one lesson that the Chinese Han people took from their long subordination to the Manchu was a fear of foreign domination and of cultural weakening. These concerns co-exist uneasily with a growing awareness of the need to embrace the creative and technological skills of non-Chinese groups in the service of nation building.

With the advent of the People's Republic of China (PRC) in 1950 there continued to be a stress on a unified ethnic nation, but there was also the beginnings of an ideological solidarity with peoples of other nations, especially the colonized peoples of Africa in their struggle for freedom (Fennell, 2013). This sense of solidarity would emphasize the commonality of the historical exploitation of China and that of peoples of color by the imperialistic and capitalist West. This resonated strongly with the Chinese's own struggles for political autonomy from the West. Despite such progressive thinking and policies, racism continued to be an issue in China with tensions and at times riots between Black students and their Chinese hosts over issues such as inter-racial dating and racial profiling by the police and immigration authorities (Hevi, 1962).

Among Chinese ethnic groups, a hierarchy tended to conflate the Han ethnic group to be representative of all Chinese groups despite the presence of minority ethnic groups. Examining relationships among indigenous Chinese ethnic groups, Myers et al. notes the dominance of the Han ethnic group that constitutes ninety percent of the Chinese population, and the wariness of the leadership to granting any substantive autonomy to minority ethnic groups. They cite statistics that indicate less than adequate outcomes concerning income, healthcare and education for most minority ethnic groups (Myers et al., 2013). Given the wariness about ethnic difference within China, it is not surprising that there would be an equally wary stance toward foreigners and resistance to them assimilating into Chinese society. It is only in recent times that China has begun to articulate an immigration policy suggesting a more tolerant stance toward non-Chinese living and working in their midst (Skeldon, 2012; China Law & Practice, 2012).

In summary, China's modern attitudes toward race are informed by the history of subjugation experienced by the now dominant Han group at the hands of the Manchu, the Europeans and the Japanese. These humiliating experiences fostered wariness toward the outsider and to non-Han ethnic groups within China. Historically, they have maintained a race-based hierarchy of peoples with themselves as the most civilized and the darker-skinned people as inferior. At the same time, they are aware of their technological inferiority in relation to the West and this led to the complex situation of wariness and a sense of cultural superiority to the West and yet an admiration of its intellectual and technological prowess.

Toward persons of Africana heritage, the perception of the Chinese has evolved over the past sixty years. What started as a relationship of solidarity in a struggle against western hegemony has evolved into one informed by multiple factors such as wariness, and yet a need for energy and minerals that are abundant in Africa and an insatiable need for individuals with technical and creative talent that increasingly includes persons of Africana heritage. The resulting up-surge of Africana migration to China has exposed many Chinese for the first time to foreigners and the attendant challenge of seeing them as human and talented in the context of a complex history of admiration, fear, contempt and at times xenophobic thinking.

The Contemporary Africana Population in China

It is difficult to get an accurate sense of the size of the Africana community in China in general and specifically in the large Africana community in southern China as no official statistics are available but unofficial estimates place the population at more than 20,000 persons (Yang, 2010; Skeldon, 2012). The Africana population is distributed mainly on China's east coast with the largest community, consisting mostly of traders, residing in Guangzhou and its environs, and a physically dispersed community of mostly corporate business professionals in Shanghai. Africana teachers of English, like students, can be found across China. The population of traders is predominantly African, unmarried young males, with Nigerians apparently comprising the largest national group (Bodomo, 2012). The trader population is quite diverse in terms of religion, ethnicity, education and migratory patterns. Some traders engage in shuttle migration, moving back and forth between home and host countries. Others are full-time residents and have Chinese wives and children born in China. Africana immigrants have access to established enclaves and communities in Guangzhou, Shanghai, Macau and to a lesser extent Beijing (Bodomo, 2012; Haugen, 2012; Morias, 2009). Many are also tightly linked to support networks in countries like Mali, Nigeria and Jamaica; places that have a long history of out migration and return.

Based on my own research, some of which is reported here, the Africana community in Shanghai is quite small and heterogeneous by country or region of origin with members from Africa and its diverse diaspora. There is no dominant ethnic or national group. This tends to be a population of well-paid and credentialed individuals, whose creative and technical skills are in high demand with many working for Chinese and international companies. It is also made up of a fair amount of teachers employed in diverse international and Chinese educational settings. The members of the Shanghai-based Africana community are for the most part formally employed, and have the legal right to live and work in China, albeit on short-term visas that must be renewed annually. This is a physically dispersed community that maintains electronic links among its members; it has a vibrant community organization that is a clearinghouse for information used to organize social events and engage in community assistance projects in Shanghai. China's oldest Africana community has existed since the seventeenth century on the former Portuguese-controlled island of Macau (Morias, 2009).

METHODOLOGY

The data for this chapter is based on fieldwork in Shanghai and Guangzhou from 2010 to 2013. Subjects were recruited through word of mouth and referrals from trusted leaders of community organizations in Shanghai and Guangzhou. I strived to interview a wide range of subjects so as to elicit a diverse range of experiences and to avoid an over representation of any one of the work groups described below. So, for example, it is relatively easy to interview traders, students and English teachers. It is harder to locate and interview artists, affluent entrepreneurs and senior executives.

The subject pool consists of forty-one individuals of Africana heritage from Africa, the Caribbean, Europe, and North America with home countries in seventeen different nation states. Twenty-three subjects were male and eighteen were female. Ages ranged from twenty one to sixty one with most subjects being in their mid-thirties. Most have resided in China for less than five years, while a few had lived there for over fifteen years. The overwhelming majority did not consider themselves fluent in Chinese but most could negotiate simple social and business transactions in Chinese. Most of the students who had been studying in Chinese universities for more than two years were literate and orally proficient in Chinese.

Subjects belonged to one of the following work groups: students, traders, entrepreneurs, English teachers, and technocrats and managers working in corporate offices. Twenty-seven subjects resided in

Shanghai, twelve subjects resided in Guangzhou and two subjects resided in small cities relatively close to Shanghai while most of the traders resided in Guangzhou. While I did not inquire directly about their immigration status in China, most immigrants described frequent trips abroad that would suggest that they had valid visas. One subject in the pool, who was a trader of modest means, had not left the country in ten years and I wondered to myself about his immigration status. Two immigrant men had Chinese wives and bicultural children born in China, but there were no Africana women in the subject pool who had Chinese husbands or partners. A few of the female subjects had Caucasian husbands or partners.

The sample described here is skewed towards university-educated subjects who have valid immigration documents and earn good salaries. They tend to be workers with formal training who are actively recruited and hired in a talent area lacking in China such as English-language proficiency, creative work or technology and so they are usually well-paid and are assisted in maintaining their immigration status. Most of the traders in the sample by contrast were small business men in an ethically challenged and cut throat business milieu with low profit margins and low levels of social trust between themselves and the Chinese, and with other Africana immigrants. They rely heavily on unscrupulous brokers to obtain and renew their visas, and must be vigilant against arbitrary arrest by the police or the immigration authorities (Haugen, 2012).

Data was collected using a structured protocol with all interviews conducted in English. Aliases were assigned and subjects were asked to discuss the attractions and constraints of their homelands with a focus on educational choices and career opportunities. Family structures and other network supports were carefully explored in the context of factors that influenced migrating to and adapting to China. Impressions of China from the perspectives of work, ethics, socializing, gender, race/ethnicity, intimacy and spirituality were explored in detail. Transcripts were analyzed based on selected themes arising from psychoanalytic and sociological perspectives on agency, structure, self and identity. The data was also analyzed using themes emerging from the psychologically attuned literature on the experience of being an immigrant.

SUBJECTS

Pseudonym	Gender	Age	Nationlity	In China	Ethnicity	Education	Occupation	Site
Dean 1	M	27	Bahamian	2008	Black	Ba-China	Trader	Gz
Chips	M	54	Nigerian	1997	Black/Tiv	Phd	Ceo	Sh
Abdoul	M	61	Guinean	1988	Fulani	Ma	Ceo	Gz
Melinda	F	40	Usa	2008	Blk-Am	Ma	Teacher	Sh
William	M	35	Bahamian	2001	Black	Ba	Designer	Sh
Sanjana	F	32	Colomb-Ian	2005	Latina	Ma-China	Sales/Mktng	Gz
John	M	35	Ugandan	2005	Mugunda	Bs	English Teacher	Gz
Cibana	M	45	Burundi	1987	Burund-Ian	Phd	Consultant	Sh
Renee	F	32	Usa	2011/7	Af Am	Masters	Corp Trainer	Sh
Omega	M	21	Usa	2012	Af Am	Undergrad	Student/Music Teacher	Sh
Krystal	F	29	Jamaican	2010	Black	Ba	English Teacher	Sao-Xing
Yoda	M	32	Am-Belgian	2006	Black	Ma	School Counselor	Sh
Harry	M	26	French	2008	French	Ba	Entrepreneur	Sh
Bill	M	39	Usa	2011	Black	Ba	English Teacher	Sh
Ojukwu	M	41	Nigerian	1997	Nnewi	College Credits	Ceo	Gz
Frank	M	41	Nigerian	2001	Igbo	Hs	Exporter	Gz

Pseudonym	Gender	Age	Nationlity	In China	Ethnicity	Education	Occupation	Site
Lama	F	29	Guinean	2006	Fulani	Hs	Exporter	Gz
Dezite	M	36	Benin	2010	Fon	Hs	Exporter	Gz
Venus	F	44	Usa	2012/2	Af Am	Ba	Lng Teacher/ Producer	Sh
Allaya	M	32	Mali	2005	Pell	Elementary	Exporter	Gz
Jay	M	38	Congo	1997	Black	Msc	Investor	Sh
Cecilia	F	33	Ugandan	2003	Blk African	Ba	Inv Advsr	Sh
Garba	M	35	Niger	2003	Blk African	Bs	Admissions Director	Sh
Elaine	F	32	Jamaican	2008	Blk Caribbean	Msc-China	English Teacher	?
Perlene	F	41	Jamaica	2009	Black	Ma En Route	Teacher	Sh
Bige	M	23	Dmnicn	2008	Black	Undergrad	Student/ Musician	Sh
Joy	F	22	Zim	2009	Blk African	Undergrad	Student	Sh
Kristina	F	46	Usa	2011/5	Af Am	Mba	Corp Trainer	Sh
Emeline	F	27		2009	Gwada/Frch	Mba	Sales Mngr	Sh
Jocelyn	M	43	Togolese	2002	Moba	Ma	Exporter	Gz
John		29	Nigerian	2012	Igbo	Ba	Exporter	Gz
Envoy	M	27	Antiguan	2009	Black	Undergrad	Student	Sh
Natasha	F	31	Jamerican	2010	Blk/Ja/Caribbean	Ma	Teacher	Sh

Pseudonym	Gender	Age	Nationlity	In China	Ethnicity	Education	Occupation	Site
Thomas	M	39	French	1994	Black	Mba	Crp Trainer/ Entrepreneur	Sh
Mikhaila	F	29	Jamaican	2009	Black	Ba	Entrepreneur	Sh
Komla	M	30	Togolese	2012/9	Ewe	Ba	Post Grad Student/ Eco	Gz
Raoul	M	35	Gwada	2002	Black	Mfa	Entrepreneur	Sh
Wei Wei	F	31	Namibian	2007	Black	Ma	Real Estate	Sh
Ann	F	29	Jamaican	2009	Jamaican	Ma	Lng Teacher	Sh
Mike	M	38	Canadian	2008	Black/Bim	Mba	It Exec	Sh
Marie	F	31	Usa	2011/1	Af Am	Mba	Student Of Chinese	Sh

RESULTS & DISCUSSION

Leaving Home

In examining the data, the focus was on the experiences of professionals, most of who were in Shanghai and some in Guangzhou. Their major motivating factor for leaving was the lack of opportunities for intellectual growth and career advancement in their respective home countries. One heard repeatedly of limited tertiary level curricula and a paucity of intellectually challenging career pipelines. While many felt they would be financially comfortable staying at home, there was a sense of a lack of intellectual growth and of substantive career mobility.

Within their respective home cultures, they reported having access to support structures that facilitate migration such as a migratory sensibility, information networks, financial resources and access to knowledgeable and welcoming enclaves in potential host countries (Bodomo, 2012; Lowenthal, 1972). These structures, when used in a thoughtful manner, enhance the migrant's sense of agency and increase the likelihood that he or she will thrive in the host culture. It also buffers him or her against the inevitable stresses of being an immigrant.

In addition, the support network at home gives the immigrant a sense of continuity and, if not too closely examined, always offers the possibility of return. Here immigrants report that they must be tactical as one of the reasons for leaving home is the restrictive and demanding nature of family. This can continue in the host country with unreasonable demand for remittances of cash and goods. Among immigrants from Africa, there was an emphasis on both material and emotional demands, while immigrants from the African diaspora in the West spoke more to the psychological demands of home. As part of their adaptive strategy, many immigrants must manage the tension between the desired aspects of home and those features that resulted in them leaving. As one migrant noted, upon returning home for a vacation, he is reminded of why he loves his country and why he chose to leave.

Many of the immigrants with professional degrees had studied and worked legally in Africa, North America and Europe, while others had travelled abroad prior to coming to China. They were somewhat disenchanted with those places, and spoke of the limited opportunities for professional growth, and especially in Europe, the lack of imaginative space. Therefore, for these immigrants, negotiating borders and being in novel locales was not really a new experience. This professional cohort is for the most part well informed and always seeking new opportunities. As such, they were attuned to reports from peers and relatives that China was the place to be. As one subject stated, "I was looking for opportunities for young people. I was happy, very happy to leave. The very first time I could make something happen [for] myself; create something in China without parental help."

REFLEXIVITY

As the above subject noted there were also psychological developmental factors at work, such as the need for autonomy and to test oneself in the world. China was thought to offer the possibility of a structural arrangement that would facilitate self-discovery and an enhanced sense of agency. The fact that an individual has migrated to China speaks to some degree to the presence of good reflective skills manifested as a need to dis-embed from structures that limit agency and embed in Chinese settings that would facilitate the growth-promoting exercise of agency. One immigrant reported that after a short stint as an English teacher in Guangzhou he found the setting too competitive, so he relocated to a third tier Chinese city where the authorities were effusive in their welcome and generous in the resources they made available to him such as housing, salary and teaching conditions. He was able to save a considerable amount of money and developed substantive relationships that enabled him to acquire better paying work than possible in Guangzhou.

Many contemporary immigrants adopt a stance of adaptive ambivalence concerning both home and host country. They find admirable and constraining qualities in both cultures. As a rule, Africana immigrants closely identify with the aesthetics (food, weather, vistas) and relationships of their homeland while bemoaning its structural limitations as manifested in the lack of opportunities for intellectual growth and access to material goods. In contrast, China is admired for the availability of resources for intellectual development and wealth acquisition. At the same time, China's questionable ethics, its polluted environment and its ambivalence toward foreigners is a source of stress.

STRUCTURE AND AGENCY

The interplay between structure and agency is quite complex and nuanced in how it is enacted in China. In response to its demand for talent, China now issues a special visa for creative workers while at the same time streamlining the processes for the enforcement of visa violations (China Law & Practice, 2012). Yet as Bodomo notes, one also observes subtle variations in how policies are enforced with regards to Africana immigrants, with an often heavy-handed approach in Guangzhou versus a more enlightened approach in Yiwu and of course the near invisibility of immigration enforcement in Shanghai (Bodomo, 2012). One effect is increased agency for a desired class of immigrants and even greater reduced agency for a less desired class of immigrant.

RELATIONS WITH THE CHINESE

Work and visa status was a crucial factor in managing relationships with the Chinese authorities. Credentialed and technically skilled individuals like those found in Shanghai, who are legally resident in China rarely, had contact with the authorities. Unlike the traders in southern China, there were no reports among them of periodic immigration sweeps or being accosted and demanded to produce proof of legal status (Bodomo, 2012; Haugen, 2012). Traders tend to work for themselves; some without documentation and whose interactions with their Chinese suppliers are mediated by cash with no requirement for the verification of their immigration status. In Shanghai the successful migrant invariably must have a legitimate visa and working papers to be employed in a well-paying job with a corporation.

The Shanghai cohort spoke of nuanced challenges in their relationship with their Chinese work colleagues. The perception of them as creative agents and their work style allow them to generate changes within the cultural structures of their workplaces. Their ideas and ways of thinking challenge some of their Chinese peers to think and act differently as creative knowledge workers. There are, however, constraints on agency within the worksite. Often there is anxiety and an accompanying resistance since many Chinese workers do not easily embrace issues of creativity and initiative to the degree that their Western counterparts do. One Africana manager reported his frustration in trying to mentor his female Chinese executive assistant. She resisted his attempts to improve her agency and told him that her job was not to think but to do simply what he told her.

For this cohort ethical interactions in the business sphere with Chinese nationals was an ongoing concern. Immigrants in this study consistently complained about Chinese indifference to honoring contracts and the tendency to try to exploit foreigners in business dealings. They spoke of a need to be vigilant and to be aggressive in such dealings; behaviors that challenged their typical ways of thinking about ethical behavior and about negotiating. While the immigrant has a wide range of opportunities to be creative and productive, there is little structural protection against unethical business practices. These ethical concerns were cited by many immigrants as being exacerbated by their race and offered this as a major reason why they would not settle permanently in China.

On a personal level, the major impediment to substantive relations between the Chinese and many of the Africana immigrants is the absence of a jointly shared language. Most immigrants are not proficient speakers of Chinese and are therefore limited to communication with English-speaking Chinese peers at work. This lack of Chinese fluency limits the ability of many Africana immigrants to engage in a socially substantive way with their Chinese peers away from the worksite; engagements that facilitate workplace understanding and creativity are not available and limit the migrant's sense of agency. When there is Chinese language competency as seen most commonly among some professionals, traders and most foreign students in China, there are reports of substantive and wide ranging relationships between the Chinese and Africana immigrants. To the extent that the migrant makes a sustained effort to learn the language and venture out of his or her ethnic enclave, there are reports of meaningful relationships with Chinese nationals.

ENCLAVES

Many in this cohort have access to enriched personal and electronically mediated networks that facilitated locating jobs and support in China. This is crucial for effective agency and mobility given that many of these knowledge workers are physically dispersed across Shanghai, Guangzhou and in the case of teachers and students across China. Given such access, they were able for the most part to avoid the numerous scams that are aimed at foreigners seeking work in China. In one case where a woman was duped, she was able to tap into a network that assisted her. These various forms of assistance rarely required monetary compensation or the use of brokers, given the quality of networks tapped, the demand for their skills and their own experiences in effectively engaging administrative systems. This is in contrast to some of the Africana traders in southern China who work for themselves, must deal with brokers, are relatively immobile, are often closely monitored, and viewed suspiciously by the law enforcement and immigration authorities (Haugen, 2012).

In speaking to Africana immigrants who work as professionals in China, they all appear to have had access to resource rich migrant networks in the home country, to its many other diasporas and access to supportive enclaves in China. Immigrants with university-level education employed in knowledge intensive industries tended to rely heavily on electronically accessible and data rich networks that provide access to jobs, housing and socializing opportunities. Given that this subgroup of immigrants tend to be physically dispersed these networks and this style of relating is vital to their cognitive and material success. It is, however, limited in its ability to address their needs for spiritual and emotional nurturance.

These enclaves are not without risk, with some immigrants reporting feeling isolated from the larger host culture. With the immigrant knowledge workers based in Shanghai the enclave is a potential bubble that encompasses Chinese colleagues who are fluent in English and are oriented toward a Western worldview. The immigrants' technical skills and Western know-how make them attractive to their English-speaking Chinese peers but such relationships often prevent them from understanding the larger culture. Most immigrants reported a tendency not to feel the need to learn Chinese and noted the limits it placed on their ability to substantially engage and understand a diverse set of Chinese nationals.

For other immigrants, the enclave is a transitional space that acts as a springboard for a deeper involvement with the host culture. They reported taking the time to cultivate relationships with Chinese peers and their families and to explore consciously outside of their expatriate, business, or school communities. Said another way, the enclave hosts many subsets of immigrants, one of which is deeply invested in understanding and being embedded in mainstream Chinese culture. Some of these immigrants strive to learn the language; some, mostly men, marry Chinese nationals and have children from those unions.

Africana immigrants also extend their sense of agency through their involvement in their own community organizations. In interviews with the leadership of the leading Nigerian community organization in Guangzhou in southern China, there was a focus on managing the perception of Africana immigrants as being prone to crime and therefore subject, at times, to harsh policing by Chinese law enforcement agencies. Community leaders devised strategies to police their nationals and to negotiate a less harsh response by the authorities. In Shanghai, the dominant immigrant community organization regularly engages in fundraising activities to assist the children of low-income Chinese internal migrants. There is no demand by its members for engagement around indigenous policing or immigration matters.

RACE

There was a consistent sense that to be of Africana heritage in China was to experience both curiosity about one's Blackness and racist behavior at the individual and institutional level. Most immigrants reported being stared and pointed at on a regular basis, and, in a personal business context, many reported being discriminated against. Africana immigrants who are native English speakers report difficulty in getting jobs as language teachers, when competing against White immigrants for whom English is a second language. For some Chinese, Whites are perceived as more competent because they are White and are initially accorded a greater degree of status and agency than that given to Africana immigrants. Others reported housing offers being withdrawn or prices for services increasing when the Chinese property owner or entrepreneur realized that the client was of Africana heritage.

At the same time, some immigrants observed that such racism was not deeply embedded and that if one was perceived as being talented then discrimination tended to be less likely. As a result, Africana immigrants recruited to work in Chinese corporations reported little evidence of racism in the workplace. It would seem that the wariness toward the foreigner in general and the Africana in general—alongside a desire for their talent—is still unresolved as reflected in visa policies and reported workplace discrimination. The tentative trend seems to be that talent and Chinese language competency trumps racism in the areas where talent is desired.

RELIGION AND INTIMACY

Chinese structures also place limits on the Africana migrant's sense of agency in terms of spirituality and intimacy. The Chinese authorities tightly regulate organized religion. While foreigners are allowed under certain circumstances to worship with Chinese nationals, there are strict guidelines that limit the degree of sermonizing that is permitted. Some immigrants who attend the officially sanctioned churches portray them as lacking theological depth and denominational specificity. The alternative is to attend "illegal" churches, which are regularly shut down by the authorities and their officiating priests are often deported (Haugen, 2011).

In the realm of intimacy, the skilled migrant is confronted, in the case of women, by the paucity of eligible male partners. Some report that Chinese men show little interest in them and the few that do want to quickly be married; non-Chinese men often act like "a child in a candy store" given their wide range of choices. Both men and women are confronted with a disadvantage arising from the sense of mobility that they prize. It means that the cadre of possible intimate partners who are fellow immigrants is always in flux given the transient nature of the foreign migrant population in China. This works against attempts to engage in substantive and enduring relationships and a potential cost of such mobility is loneliness (Strenger, 2013).

CONCLUSION

While China is experiencing high demand for creative workers, it is still establishing the necessary structures to accommodate fully their need for personal fulfillment that goes beyond intellectually challenging work and material rewards. Still unresolved is the marked tension between the antipathy to foreigners and an admiration of, and desire for, their technical skills. For Africana immigrants, China is a site of opportunity and risk that leaves many in a position of adaptive ambivalence. In the context of an unblinking assessment of the pleasures and deficits of their home countries, they appreciate and take advantage of the opportunities that China offers in the intellectual and wealth acquisition spheres. They are also keenly aware of its ethical shortcomings, its unsafe environment and products, and the structural constraints that make the pursuit of spirituality and intimacy challenging. At the same time, Africana immigrants with their enhanced sense of agency are challenging extant Chinese ways of thinking, resulting in structural changes in areas such as immigration policy, the response to creative workers, and in law enforcement. One can conclude that migration in a globalized world might offer economic and intellectual benefits but the psychosocial aspects of agency are under-thematized and the results here suggest that they can be quite costly even for seemingly well-qualified immigrants.

REFERENCES

Akyeampong, Emmanuel (2000) "Africans in the Diaspora: The Diaspora of Africa." *African Affairs* 99 : 193-215.

Bakewell, Oliver (2010) "Some Reflections on Structure and Agency in Migration Theory." *Journal of Ethnic and Migration Studies* 36.10 : 1689-1708.

Bodomo, Adams (2012) "African Students in China: A Case Study of Newly Arrived Students on FOCAC Funds at Chongqing University." *The University of Hong Kong. Web. Retrieved on 15th January 2012 from http://wwwo.hku.hk/cerc/Seminars/African_Students_in_ChinaChongqing.pdf

—. (2010) The African trading community in Guangzhou: An emerging bridge for Africa-China relations. *The China Quarterly* 203, 693-707.

—. (2012) *Africans in China: A Sociocultural Study and its Implication for Africa-China Relations.* Amherst, N.Y: Cambria Press.

Castles, Steven (2010) "Understanding Global Migration: A Social Transformative Perspective." *Journal of Ethnic and Migration Studies* 36.10, 1565-1586.

China Law & Practice. (2012) *"China's New Immigration Law Explained."* China Law and Practice, 2012. Web. Retrieved on 12 January 2013 from http://www.chinalawandpractice.com/Article /3060403/Channel/9931/Chinas-new-Immigration-Law-explained.html

Davin, Delia. (1998) *Internal Migration in Contemporary China.* Basingstoke, England: Macmillan Press.

—. (2009) "Internal Migration in China." *DevISSues: DevelopmentISSues* 11.2 (November 2009): 13-15. Web. Retrieved on 21 May 2014 from http://www.iss.nl/fileadmin/ASSETS/iss/Documents/DevISSues/DevIS-Sues11_2_Nov_09_web.pdf

Dikotter, Frank. (1992) *The Discourse of Race in Modern China.* London: Hurst & Company.

Farrer, J. (2010). "New Shanghailanders' or 'New Shanghainese': Western Expatriates' Narratives of Emplacement in Shanghai." *Journal of Ethnic and Migration Studies* 2010: 1-18.

Fei, Wu. (2011) "Suicide, a Modern Problem in China." In Arthur Kleinman, Yunxiang Yan, Jing Jun, Sing Lee, Everett Zhang, Pan Tianshu, Wu Fei and Guo Jinhau (Eds.), *Deep China: The Moral Life of the Person, What Anthropology and Psychiatry Tell Us About China Today*, pp. 212-236. Berkeley, CA: University of California Press.

Fennell, V. (2013) "Race: China's Question and Problem." *Review of Black Political Economy* 40, 245-275.

Florida, Richard. (2002) *The Rise of the Creative Class.* New York: Basic Books.

Haugen, H. (2011). *African Pentecostal Immigrants in China: Urban Marginality and Alternative Geographies of a Mission Theology.* Paper presented at the International RC21 conference 2011: Session 9: "Invisible immigrants in the cities of the South." *UNESCO.* 2011.Web. Retrieved on 21 January 2013 from http://www.unescochair-iuav.it/wp-content/uploads/2010/12/rc21-african-pentecostal-migrants-in-china.pdf

—. "Nigerians in China: A Second State of Mobility." *International Migration* 50.2 (2012): 65-80.

Hevi, Emmanuel J. (1963) *An African student in China.* New York: Frederick Praeger Publishers.

Hitlin, S., & Elder, Jr. G (2007) "Time, Self, and the Curiously Abstract Concept of Agency." *Sociological Theory* 25.2, 170-191.

Hui, Wang (2009) *The End of the Revolution: China and the Limits of Modernity.* Brooklyn, NY: Verso.

Jayasuriya, Shihan. (2006) "Identifying Africans in Asia: What's in a Name?" *African and Asian Studies,* 5.3-4, 275-303.

Johnson, M. Dujon. (2011) *Race & Racism in the Chinas: Chinese Racial Attitudes toward Africans and African-Americans.* Bloomington, IN: Authorhouse.

Kleinman, Arthur., Yan,Yunxiang., Jun Jing., Lee, Sing., Zhang, Everett., Tianshu, Pan., Fei, Wu., Jinhua, Guo (2011) *"Deep China: The Moral Life of the Person,"* What Anthropology and Psychiatry Tell Us about China Today.* Berkley, CA: University of California Press.

Lowenthal, David (1972) *West Indian Societies.* New York: Oxford University Press.

Lu, Yao & Zhou, Hao (2013) "Academic Achievement and Loneliness of Migrant Children in China: School Segregation and Segmented Assimilation." *Comparative Education Review* 57.1, 85-116.

Matthews, Gordon. (2011) *Ghetto at the Center of the World: Chungking Mansions.* Chicago, IL: University of Chicago Press.

Mitter, Rana (2004) *A Bitter Revolution: China's Struggle with the Modern World.* New York: Oxford University Press.

Morais, Isabel. (2009) "China 'Wahala': The tribulations of Nigerian 'Bushfallers' in a Chinese territory." *Journal of Global Cultural Studies* 5: 2-22. Web. Retrieved on 5 February 2012 from http://transtexts.revues.org/281

Myers, Samuel L., Xiaoyan, Gau, Cruz, Britt (2013) "Ethnic Minorities, Race, and Inequality in China: A New Perspective on Racial Dynamics." *Review of Black Political Economy* 40: 231-244.

Sewell, Jr. William H. (1992) "A Theory of Structure: Duality, Agency, and Transformation." *American Journal of Sociology* 98.1: 1-29.

Simpson, Nicole (2013) "Happiness and Migration." In, Amelie Constant & Klaus Zimmerman (Eds.) *International Handbook on the Economics of Migration*, pp. 393-407, Northampton, MA: Edward Elgar Publishing. *Institute for the Study of Labor*. Web. Retrieved on 14 May 2014 from http://www.iza.org/MigrationHandbook/21_Simpson_Happiness%20and%20Migration.pdf

Skeldon, Ronald. (2012). *"China: An Emerging Destination for Economic Migration."* *Migration Information*. 2012. Web. Retrieved on 22 February 2012 from http://www.migrationinformation.org/Profiles/display.cfm?ID=838

Solinger, Dorothy J. (1999) "Citizen's Issues in China's Internal Migration: Comparisons with Germany and Japan." *Political Science Quarterly* 114.3: 455-478.

Spence, Jonathan D. (1990). *The Search for Modern China*. New York: W.W. Norton & Company, 1990.

Strenger, C. (2013) "The New Cosmopolitans: Challenges and Discontents." *Psychoanalytic Psychology* 30.2: 264-280.

Taylor, Guy. (2007) "Migration Studies Unit Working Papers: China's Floating Immigrants: Updates from the 2005 1% Population Sample Survey." *London School of Economics and Political Science*. 2007.Web. . Retrieved on 23 June 2014 from http://www.lse.ac.uk/government/research/resgroups/MSU/documents/workingPapers/WP_2011_07.pdf

Wyatt, Don J. (2010) *The Blacks of Pre-Modern China*. Philadelphia, PA: University of Philadelphia Press.

Xiao, Y., Zhao, N., Yu, M., Zhao, M., Zhong, J., Gong, W., Hu, R. (2013) "Factors Associated with Severe Deliberate Self-Harm among Chinese Internal Migrants." *PLOS: One*. 2013. Web. Retrieved on 15 July 2014 from http://www.plosone.org/article/info%3Adoi%2F10.1371%2Fjournal.pone.0080667

Yan, Yunxiang. "The Changing Moral Landscape." In, Arthur Kleinman, Yan Yunxiang, Jun Jing, Lee Sing, Everett Zhang (2011) *Deep China: The Moral Life of the Person, What Anthropology and Psychiatry Tell Us about China Today*, p, 36-77. Berkeley, CA: University of California Press.

Yang, Yang (2010) *"African Traders in Guangzhou, China: Routes, Profits and Reasons."* *The Chinese University of Hong Kong.* Web. Retrieved on 29 January 2012 from http://www.cuhk.edu.hk/ant/PostgraduateForum2011/Econ/YANGYang.pdf

AFRICAN UNIVERSITY STUDENTS IN CHINA'S HONG KONG: MOTIVATIONS, ASPIRATIONS AND FURTHER EXCHANGES[1]

CHAK-PONG GORDON TSUI

INTRODUCTION

This chapter explores the motivations and aspirations of African students who choose Hong Kong as their destination for university studies. Based on the findings of in-depth interviews with ten African students in Hong Kong, this chapter postulates that academic reputation and financial incentives are the two main motivations for attending university in Hong Kong. Other factors such as good teaching, research supervision, and treating Hong Kong as a stepping-stone to China also motivate some students. However, this chapter identifies a general pattern that indicates most of the African students do not intend to stay in Hong Kong after graduation. While internationalization is a major strategic development of Hong Kong universities, there remains an insignificant number of African students on Hong Kong campuses. The chapter suggests that recruiting more African university students can enhance the international profile of Hong Kong universities and strengthen academic internationalization at large.

More than half a century ago, the academic literature on the university destinations of African students began to emerge with particular interest in the case of the United States (Banks, 2006). Yet thus far, studies on African students in Hong Kong are almost non-existent, largely due to its comparatively small population size. The population of international students at The University of Hong Kong, for instance, has a skewed nationality distribution. There is an obvious contrast in population size between the dominant group of Mainland Chinese students and the minority groups of African students and South American students—which constitute less than one percent of the total student population (The University of Hong Kong, 2012a).[2] This continuous under-representation of African students raises an interesting question: What motivates this small but emerging student group to come to this post-colonial Chinese city? This question is important given that this initial batch of students may expand networks by sharing experiences and thereby potentially motivating subsequent batches of African students to consider Hong Kong as a destination for their university studies. Considering this issue, this chapter will firstly review the relevant literature. Secondly, it will discuss the methodological tools used to answer the research questions. The third section will examine the results of interviews with ten African students in Hong Kong. Lastly, the key issues and implications for further research will be discussed in-depth.

AFRICAN STUDENTS IN CHINA'S HONG KONG: THE CONTEXT

Cooperation between Africa, China, and Hong Kong dates back to the establishment of the People's Republic of China in 1949. But the scale and substance of such cooperation have undergone a significant transformation over time (Gillespie, 2001). The early China-led political cooperation helped former colonized African countries to tackle political crisis, namely by claiming that both parties were part of the "Third World" (Gillespie, 2001: 20). Tighter Africa-China exchanges have become increasingly based around economic issues, especially in the aftermath of the 2007-08 financial crises (Bodomo, 2012). But an academic element has also turned out to be prevalent in the Africa-China interactions when the increasing trend of African students studying in China is considered.

Bodomo (2012) argues that, in general, Africa could not be fully interpreted as a single entity because some African countries had closer relations to China than others (Bodomo, 2009). In addition, he argues that migration for most of the Africans to Hong Kong is driven by economic incentives, whereas only two out of thirty participants in his research came to Hong Kong with an academic pursuit (Bodomo, 2012). Meanwhile, the research site (at the ChungKing Mansions on Nathan Road in Hong Kong) has been negatively described as "dangerous [and] unsafe" (Bodomo, 2006: 457) and is often seen as a place where people are obsessed with "drugs [and] crimes" (Bodomo, 2006: 457). Furthermore, the area of African students in Hong Kong is under-researched according to the related academic literatures.

To explain the motivations and aspirations of international students, Mpingganjira categorizes the factors into academic, personal, and occupational dimensions. Generally speaking, international students are motivated academically by the "high quality of education abroad," personally by the "want to broaden personal experience" and occupationally by perceiving that "studying abroad can enhance future employment" (2009: 361). Regarding the ethnoscape of international students, Altbach and Knight observe a "South to North" flow (Altbach and Knight, 2007: 28). In this connection, Phelps (2010) adds that many international students are from less developed countries due to the significant differences between the quality of university education provided by the developed countries and the developing counterparts.

As for Africa, there are on average less than six universities in each country—approximately 300 universities across 55 African countries (Teferra & Altbach, 2004). Teferra and Altbach (2004) argue that African universities are relatively novices in operation and in delivering quality teaching and research, not unrelated to the economic (under)development. Lack of university places and shortage of quality education are the factors that push African students to study abroad. However, it is not accurate to over-generalize that the overall African higher education system is disadvantaged, given that some countries are doing exceptionally better than others. Notable examples include Egyptian higher education as one of the oldest in the world, the increasing higher education enrollment rates in Nigeria and South Africa, and the growth of "private higher education" in Kenya (Teferra & Altbach, 2004 :31). Moreover, Muuka and Choongo (2009) argue that with the development of solid quality assurance measures (for students, teachers and areas of study), Africa is the continent with the highest potential for growth, particularly in terms of global influence. Yet, these are in initial stages and the outcomes are yet to be determined. Uneven resource distribution in some African universities, including the funding imbalance between undergraduates and postgraduates (for example in law faculties), motivates some postgraduate students to opt for a place in overseas universities, with the UK and the US being the most popular countries (Mwenda, 2009). Furthermore, overseas education is likely to be more beneficial when the students aim for a career in the political field (Constant et al., 2010). Therefore disciplinary consideration and career aspiration are the important factors that shape the ethnoscape of African overseas students' migration.

African students *de facto* constitute the largest proportion among the international students in the UK (Maringe & Carter, 2007). As the former colonizer of a significant portion of the African continent, the UK is a popular destination for many African students largely due to the strong linkage and transferability in terms of academic structure, education qualifications and academic culture between the British system and its African counterpart. In the US, African students are however not the dominant group (Aslanbeigui & Montecinos, 1998), although more African students can be found in some departments, such as computer science, at the graduate level (Hazen & Alberts, 2006). A strong likelihood is that most African students will go back to their home countries after graduation (Hazen & Albert, 2006). Regarding the case of Asia, Bodomo (2012) notes the growing number of African students studying in China and most of them study on scholarship or other financial sponsorship. As for Hong Kong, internationalization is still a top issue on the university's agenda (see The University of Hong Kong, 2012b & The University of Hong Kong, 2015b), and research about African students on Hong Kong campuses will add important knowledge to the academic literature and inform university policies. On top of the issues we discussed above, the gender issue of African overseas students is a special point of interest in this topic. According to Maundeni (1999), African women are assumed to play the role of family helpers and African female students are often disadvantaged under the dominance of male African students. This chapter will revisit this point when the research sampling and implications are discussed.

RESEARCH QUESTIONS

Based on the context of African students in Hong Kong, this chapter aims to investigate the following areas:

1. Motivations: What motivates African students to come to Hong Kong for their higher education studies?

2. Adaptations and Universities' Support: How do African students adapt to life in Hong Kong? Do Hong Kong universities provide sufficient support?

3. Aspirations: What are the aspirations of African students after they have completed their course of study in Hong Kong?

METHODOLOGY

This chapter employed in-depth interviews as the main research method. The author of this chapter conducted the interviews between May and June 2013 in his capacity as a local postgraduate student at The University of Hong Kong. The interview data are supplemented by related survey data (Miles and Huberman, 1994). Owing to the small number of African students in Hong Kong, in-depth case studies are a more appropriate method to investigate the uniqueness of every participant. For example, African students were only included in the category of "others" which includes "Central and South America and African Countries," constituting a total share of 0.9 percent (The University of Hong Kong, 2012a). Also, interviews can comprehensively identify the gradual changes of each participant over time by the interviewer asking about their experiences and life history at different stages of their studies (Miles & Huberman, 1994). A quantitative survey was utilized at an earlier stage to identify participants' demographic information, within which some variables could be observed to support the interview data (Wolf, 1997). For data interpretation, the interviews were audio-recorded and subsequently coded to identify the core emerging themes and patterns from the transcripts (Miles & Huberman, 1994). All data were cross-checked by the interviewees to ensure data consistency and credibility. The demographic information of the ten research participants (each of them is identified with codes from RP001 to RP010) can be found in Table 1.

TABLE I : PROFILE OF THE RESEARCH PARTICIPANTS (RPS)

Research Participant	Country of Origin	British Connection	Gender	Marital Status	Overseas Experience Before Hong Kong	Age	Study Major
RP001	Eritrea	Former British Colony	Male	Married	Yes [UK]	40 or above	Education
RP002	Egypt	Former British Colony	Male	Single	Yes [Germany]	20-29	Computer Science
RP003	Ghana	Former British Colony	Male	Single	Yes [UK]	30-39	Construction Management
RP004	Ghana	Former British Colony	Male	Married	No	30-39	Journalism
RP005	Kenya	Former British Colony	Male	Single	Yes [UK]	20-29	Law
RP006	Nigeria	Former British Colony	Male	Single	Yes [US, Greece]	20-29	Information Systems
RP007	Nigeria	Former British Colony	Male	Single	No	20-29	Computer Science
RP008	Nigeria	Former British Colony	Male	Single	No	30-39	Building and Real Estate
RP009	Tanzania	Former British Colony	Male	Married	No	40 or above	Education
RP010	Zimbabwe	Former British Colony	Male	Married	No	30-39	Sociology

FINDINGS

Explorative in nature, this research sought to identify the individual motivations through in-depth interviews. The interview data are reported according to key themes and conceptual issues. Academic factors can be identified as the most common and important considerations for the decision to study in Hong Kong. According to one interviewee, "Hong Kong is a good place and when I graduate from Hong Kong, I can compete with anyone in the world—from Oxford, from Sydney, from America and even from Africa."[3] This reflects the participant's confidence about his studies as competitive as other globally renowned universities. RP003 articulated the quality of higher education offered in Hong Kong in the following way: "The training and access to resources are special, because it is difficult to do a PhD in my country. For instance, even though you get professors who have studied abroad, the resources are not up to the standard, compared with the resources that I will get in places like HKU."[4]

Various aspects of the quality of education that Hong Kong universities offered were discussed in several interviews. "For the motivation to come to Hong Kong," noted one student (RP009), "it was, like, to get more exposure, to get more experience of a developed university… because if you think about the university I am studying at right now, it is very much more competitive compared with those in developing countries."[5] For another (RP002), "The university ranking is very well-known in the world, so everybody is watching the University of Hong Kong. For the technical level, I think it is a very promising topic regarding the new future design of computers and operating systems."[6] Others found their department to be central: "If you look at the staff component within the department at HKU, you find out that it is a mainly cosmopolitan kind of society where you see professors, lecturers, and researchers from different places across the world."[7] Another student (RP004) affirmed this observation: "I notice that almost all my lecturers in my department, almost all of them come from different backgrounds. They are not only from China; they are from different parts of the world. So, that also brings together a whole experience of academic background and that is very important to me."[8]

The above interview data illustrate the competitive edges that Hong Kong universities possess as most of them aim to provide an international platform for their students (see The University of Hong Kong, 2012b). Supervision by excellent academic professionals is undoubtedly an attractive point for those seeking a research postgraduate degree in Hong Kong. Hong Kong's reputation, with its well-developed university sector, has gained currency worldwide (Tang, 2014). According to Mpingganjira (2009), access to high quality education abroad is one of the justifications for overseas studies. International students also perceive that future employment prospects can be enhanced by studying abroad (Mpingganjira, 2009). In this connection, RP001 stated, "I met people from Singapore, from India, from Malaysia, from other countries and I asked them whether it was good to go and study at The University of Hong Kong. They strongly recommended me to go and do my studies at The University of Hong Kong."[9] Further, RP004 reported, "So if you happen to graduate from The University of Hong Kong with a Master's Degree, I mean everybody would know that you are a good student."[10]

This reputation, not surprisingly, is constructed through the "social technology" of first-rate university rankings of different sorts. RP010 reinforces this point: "I always have this admiration for the University of Hong Kong because I have seen in particular how the University of Hong Kong... say for ranking... is one of the top universities in the world."[11] Likewise, RP007 noted, "It is a fact that I noticed and saw that the University of Hong Kong, in some of the rankings, was ranked 21st/22nd and indeed was ranked the first university in Asia. I said wow; this must be a giant in Asia."[12] Indeed, expectation for Hong Kong's reputation can also be one motivation. RP006 and RP009 reported, "And then generally I think City U is on the path of progress especially in world university rankings. Maybe three years ago, it was 130th... something like 135th, and right now it is 95th and I see that it is going upwards, I think it is an extremely remarkable progress for a university of less than 30 years old."[13] Some disciplines were noted as performing particularly well in the rankings. As RP001 remarks, "The Faculty of Education has a very high reputation in this area."[14] Indeed, the respondents perceived this would prove to be extremely useful in terms of "marketing" themselves in the future. RP009 concurred: "When I get an education at The University of Hong Kong, I would get a fantastic education which would be very marketable."[15]

The Global Currency of Hong Kong Academic Credentials

In terms of academic credentials, a Hong Kong degree was perceived as putting African students in an advantageous position with high global currency. RP009 tells us: "You will be widening the possibilities of getting more jobs elsewhere in the world because people would think about where this guy is coming from...he graduated from this university!"[16] Furthermore, according to RP003, "I knew about HKU because I already knew two people from my department back in my country who came to do their PhD at HKU. You know, sometimes I just search from university rankings... The University really has quite a number of the staff from around the world, so that would be a good environment, too."[17] RP009 also revealed, with reference to a friend who graduated with a PhD from a Hong Kong university, the following: "Why they wanted to hire him was not only because he had a PhD. No, it was because he got a PhD from a reputable university. It is not just getting a PhD from any universities."[18] Alongside the findings in the previous sections, interview data continued to buttress the idea that overseas education can enhance future employment (Mpingganjira, 2009) and that it gives students a promising future after graduation.

Overseas Experience Prior to Hong Kong and the British Connections and Legacy

It is noteworthy that all participants were from former British colonies and most of the ten students in this study had overseas experience, especially in the UK, prior to their studies in Hong Kong. In describing the ethos of a Hong Kong University, RP002 explicitly stated, "I feel like Hong Kong has a very British style."[19] The use of English as a research and teaching language encourages the movement of African students to universities in Hong Kong. RP003 stated, "It was the fact that in HKU the official language of the University [is English]. So at least, I get to talk to my supervisor in English and, you know, also with some colleagues and other staff."[20] RP004 further elaborated: "And also the fact that it is mainly an English-speaking university. I wouldn't have that kind of language barrier to studying and that was the first motivation which brought me to The University of Hong Kong."[21] For RP006, the encounter of East and West made Hong Kong "a place where you can have a feeling of the real Eastern cultures like Chinese culture, but at the same time, you can feel Western influences in the city, as it was a British colony for a long time. It still has the British influence here. The official languages are actually English and Cantonese."[22] Echoing Zaccrisson's (2004) argument that English is an influential factor for overseas studies, the findings presented above highlight the fact that the influence of English is not only in the realm of language, but also in terms of culture. African students can find the British colonial legacy displayed in the key elements of Hong Kong's culture. This could explain Hong Kong as their final choice of their studies.

International Networks and Exposure in Hong Kong Universities

International networks and international exposure offered by Hong Kong universities are essential features that motivate students from Africa to come to study in Hong Kong. RP006 expressed this idea as follows: "We have a lot of very famous professors here, for example, the leader of the Association of Information Systems, which is pretty much the biggest information systems organization in the world."[23] In the same token, as expressed by RP004, "It has been a good stepping-stone for me, a point where I feel that I can reach out to the rest of the world to do anything that I want to do. With my chest out, I am very confident of what I have to do."[24] Indeed, according to RP009, international exposure in academic work is extremely important: "You need to be part of a society, which has reputable researchers. So if you get the wide knowledge offered by

The University of Hong Kong, I hope it would let someone get much more exposure, much more exposed to the academic point of view, exposure in terms of research and making links to others you know around the world because this university is highly linked. So many people from different parts of the world come here."[25] Overall, Hong Kong universities are on par with other exceptional universities, offering similar scope and substance of international exposure and networks for the benefit of graduates' future career (Hazen & Alberts, 2006).

Financial Support and Time to Complete Degree

The financial support enjoyed by the full time research postgraduate students in Hong Kong is an important factor in the African students' consideration and calculation to come to Hong Kong. RP009 revealed, "If you get an offer in my country, your offer will be around 6,000 Hong Kong dollars [per month]. You do not need to pay that much per month, out of that you have to pay your school fee, university fee. But at HKU, at the point I joined this university, they were offering me around 13,000 [per month]."[26] RP006 believed stable and sufficient financial support enabled him to concentrate on his studies, making his studies more efficient: "It is more work but I always love challenges and I think my coming to Hong Kong was also quite attractive—in that I could get it [doctoral study] done in three or four years and all the things in my life here look good."[27] A similar point was expressed by RP003: "I applied to one other university not in Hong Kong and I got admission as well. They all gave me admission but it came to who gave me funding, it was down to who gave me funding... I got funding for four years because I didn't really want to do a PhD with half funding [from a UK university]."[28]

In comparative terms, the financial incentive provided by Hong Kong universities is considerably attractive. For RP001, "Apart from the quality of the education in Hong Kong, I found out that the situation about the tuition fees was very fair, especially when I compare that I can get the same quality of education that I would get in the UK, but the kind of fees that I am paying here are much cheaper."[29] Findings from this research and the academic literature show that financial incentive is evident in motivating overseas education. Phelps (2010) argues that the flow of international students is more often from less developed countries to the more developed ones, instead of the other way round. In this case, the migration flow of African university students to the economically better off Hong Kong agrees with the general argument of relevant studies (cf. Bodomo, 2012).

Different Takes on Being Mobile: Married Students and Single Students

Concerning the strategies for being mobile, the African participants differ according to their marital status. RP009 described family as a source of motivation for pursuing higher education studies: "If you have a family before you come to study, the family wants you to get to a higher level of education, that might give you pressure... They need my support. So, with these needs, they really motivate me to go back to stay with my family."[30] The view of RP001, who is also a married student, echoes this sentiment: "People like me who are married, who have some responsibilities back at home do need to keep in touch with the family because it makes you to be at ease in your study and you can fully concentrate on your studies. If, however, you do not have access to your family, it is [somewhat] frustrating. You always get worried about your family back at home. It really affects the motivations that I have contact on a regular base with my family... you are keeping in touch with your family on a regular basis, this means whatever the decision you make, it is becoming a shared decision, for example, after your graduation, you have to decide whether you go back home, whether you stay here and work in Hong Kong or whether you go somewhere else. You can discuss this sort of thing on a daily basis with your family and you decide together, so it is really helpful."[31] Most of the research participants for this chapter do not intend to stay in Hong Kong upon graduation. The general intention of returning to Africa implies that their stay in Hong Kong is temporary, treating the destination of higher education as a stepping-stone (Hazen and Alberts, 2012).

DISCUSSION

A combination of factors motivated the students to come to Hong Kong. RP006's statement is probably the most convincing to explain the situation for the limited number of African students in Hong Kong: "We do not conventionally come to a place like Hong Kong to study. Usually the destinations of choice include the UK, the US, and some parts of Europe but not really Hong Kong."[32] Some participants for this research had indeed studied overseas (e.g. the UK and the US) before coming to Hong Kong. Still, Hong Kong was chosen as their current education destination because Hong Kong was the most internationalized city within the Chinese region, and the financial sponsorship offered by Hong Kong universities was more attractive than other polities in the region. The relatively shorter time to complete the degree in Hong Kong also suits some students. All of these points allow Hong Kong universities to be unique in motivating the participants to study in Hong Kong. In addition, the British influence seemed to have motivated RP010 and other students' selection of Hong Kong universities. Nevertheless, motivations were different between two groups: the married and the unmarried students. The first group had a higher tendency to go back to their country upon graduation. Contrasting views can be gauged by the following two pieces of interview data: "I don't think I will be able to stay behind after graduation without my family here" and "not much actually, but I keep in contact with my family, we keep talking. But family was never the top priority of my decision to come to Hong Kong."[33]

On another point, most participants expressed the fact that they were academically motivated to study in Hong Kong in the first place. However, some participants revealed that social needs were gradually found to be essential for sustaining a good study life. For example, RP009, who was in his final stage of PhD studies, explained that the longer he stayed in Hong Kong, the more important social life became as it made his study life more satisfying. This indicates that academic factors motivate some African students to come to Hong Kong, but socio-cultural factors have often become increasingly important as they establish themselves in Hong Kong.

CONCLUSION, RESEARCH IMPLICATIONS AND LIMITATIONS

Academic reputation was the most important motivating factor for African students to choose Hong Kong universities, although other factors contributed to this final choice. Other factors such as family and social interactions also affected their motivations after settling in Hong Kong. Overall, their motivations were generally similar, despite certain personal characteristics and perspectives.

As an exploratory study, this chapter has offered some preliminary and informative findings but the limited number of participants means that it cannot make wider generalizations about the motivations of African students who choose Hong Kong universities. In particular, all the participants were 1) males, 2) postgraduates, and 3) from former British colonies; the research was specific enough to shed light on this group of students. Still, what the term "African university students" covers is very general. Other, very different, groups could include African females, undergraduates, and Africans from non-former British colonies, which were not investigated.

It is suggested that further research is undertaken to investigate overseas African students. The scope of the student population could be extended, for example, to females and undergraduates. This is because the literature has shown that African women are often disadvantaged, whereas motivations, academic experiences and aspirations of undergraduates and postgraduates are expected to be largely different (e.g. Manudeni, 1999). In addition, family issues were found to be a highly important factor for making sense of the students' motivations and aspirations for overseas studies. Finally, a reconsideration of the "West" at the center of higher education is necessary. On this point, RP001 noted, "People have the mentality that the best education in the world can be found mainly in the western countries. I really want to challenge that as you can get the same kind of quality education in some Asian countries such as Hong Kong."[34]

Future research might further test whether Hong Kong's reputation as a center for world class higher education as well as the global currency of Hong Kong academic credentials remain as the key motivating factors for African students to study in Hong Kong.

Preliminary insights offered by this chapter may inform further studies about the African presence in emerging higher education hubs, especially those not located in the West, but in different parts of the world. To enable students from Hong Kong universities to understand the presence of African students, the author has been organizing a number of African service learning trip with a Hong Kong African student every year since his Masters studies in 2013 to seek further exchanges with Africa. It is hoped that the exchanges can serve as one direction of further research.

REFERENCES

Altbach, P. G., & Knight, J. (2007). The internationalization of higher education: motivations and realities. *The NEA 2006 Almanac of Higher Education, 11* (3-4), 27-36.

Aslanbeigui, N., & Montecinos, V. (1998). Foreign students in U.S. doctoral programs. *The Journal of Economic Perspectives, 12*(3), 171-182.

Banks, J. A. (2006). *Race, Culture, and Education: The Selected Works of James A. Banks.* London; New York: Routledge.

Bodomo, A. (2006). An Emerging African-Chinese Community in Hong Kong: The case of Tsim Sha Tsui's Chungking Mansions. In K. K. Prasad & J.-P. Angenot (Eds.) *TADIA The African Diaspora in Asia.* (pp. 445-460). Bangalore: Tadia Society.

Bodomo, A. (2009). Africa-China relations: Symmetry, soft power and South Africa, *The China Review: An Interdisciplinary Journal on Greater China, 9*(2), 169-178.

Bodomo, A. (2012). *Africans in China: A Sociocultural Study and Its Implications on Africa-China Relations.* Amherst. NY: Cambria Press.

Constant, Amelie, F., Tien, & N, B. (2010). African leaders: Their education abroad and FDI flows, Discussion Paper. *German Institute for Economic Research, No. 1087,* 1-27.

Gillespie, S. (2001). China's Changing World View: The Evolution of Foreign Policy During the Maoist Reign. In E. Beauchamp (Ed.), *South-South Transfer: A Study of Sino-African exchanges* (pp.7-26). New York: Routledge.

Hazen, H. D., & Alberts, H. C. (2006). Visitors or immigrants? International students in the United States, *Population, Space and Place, 12*(3), 201-216.

Hornby, A. S. (2004). *Oxford Advanced Learner's English-Chinese Dictionary.* (7th ed). Hong Kong: Oxford University Press, p.1128.

Maringe, F., & Catrer, S. (2007). International students' motivations for studying in UK HE: Insights into the choice and decision making of African students. *International Journal of Educational Management, 21*(6), 459-475.

Maundeni, T. (1999). African females and adjustment to studying abroad. *Gender and Education, 11*(1), 27-42.

Miles, M. B., & Huberman, A. M. (1994), *An Expanded Sourcebook Qualitative Data Analysis* (2nd ed.). Thousand Oaks: Sage Publications.

Mpingganjira, M. (2009). Comparative analysis of factors influencing the decision to study abroad, *African Journal of Business Management, 3*(8). 358-365.

Muuka, G. N., & Choongo, M. M. (2009). The challenge of African journalism education in the age of global terrorism. In K. K. Mwenda & G. N. Muuka (Eds.) *The Challenge of Change in Africa's Higher Education in the 21st Century* (2nd ed.) (pp. 195-223). Amherst, N.Y.: Cambia Press.

Mwaura, J. N. (2008). *Black African International Adult Students' Experiences in Higher Education: A Qualitative Study* (Doctoral dissertation, The Pennsylvania State University).

Mwenda, K. K. (2009). Developing academic degree programs in Commonwealth African law schools: Lessons from the British and American legal education system. In K. K. Mwenda & G. N. Muuka (Eds.) *The Challenge of Change in Africa's Higher Education in the 21st Century* (2nd ed.) (pp. 81-131). Amherst, N.Y.: Cambia Press.

Phelps, C. E. (2010). Bringing international students to campus: Who, what, when, where, why and how? In D. B. Johnstone, M. d'Ambrosio & P. J. Yakoboski (Eds.) *Higher Education in a Global Society* (pp.162-183). Cheltenham, UK; Northampton, MA: Edward Elgar.

Tang, H.H.H. (2014). Academic capitalism in Greater China: Theme and variations. In Brendan Cantwell and Ilkka Kauppinen (Eds.), *Academic Capitalism in the Age of Globalization* (pp.208-227). Baltimore, Maryland: The Johns Hopkins University Press.

Teferra, D., & Altbach, P. G. (2004). African higher education: Challenges for the 21st century. *Higher Education, 47* (1), 21-50.

The University of Hong Kong. (2012a). Student Profiles 2011/2012 (In Headcounts) In *Quick Stats.* Retrieved 18 Feb, 2013 from *http://www.cpao.hku.hk/qstats/student-profiles*

The University of Hong Kong. (2012b). Why HKU In *International Students Admission.* Retrieved 17 Feb, 2013 from http://www.als.hku.hk/admission/intl/international-recognition

The University of Hong Kong. (2015a). Student Profiles 2014/2015 (In Headcounts) In *Quick Stats.* Retrieved 6 Dec, 2015 from http://www.cpao.hku.hk/qstats/student-profiles

The University of Hong Kong. (2015b). Why HKU In *International Students Admission.* Retrieved 6, Dec, 2015 from http://www.als.hku.hk/admission/intl/international-recognition

Wolf, R. M. (1997). Questionnaire. In J. P. Keeves (Ed.), *Educational Research, Methodology, and Measurement: An International Handbook* (2nd ed.) (pp. 422-426). New York, N.Y: Pergamon.

Zachrisson, C. U. (2004). New study abroad destinations: Trends and emerging opportunities, *Europe, 76*, 62-67.

SOME EMPIRICAL AND METHODOLOGICAL PROBLEMS FOR CALIBRATING THE AFRICAN PRESENCE IN GREATER CHINA

ADAMS BODOMO AND CAROLINE PAJANCIC

INTRODUCTION

In the last 10 years, much research has gone into finding answers to key questions about the African presence in Greater China (mainland China, Hong Kong, Macau and Taiwan). We now have answers to such questions as why Africans go to China, the major cities Africans visit and live, what they do there, and how they are received by the Chinese state and the Chinese people. What has, however, been elusive to date is calculating fairly exact or accurate numbers for Africans in China. Apart from issues about the usefulness of such an enterprise, there are a number of reasons that make this an arduous task, including the fact that accurate official records hardly exist on the numbers of foreigners in China, the preponderance of "qualitative" research does not allow for accurate extrapolations of Africans in China based on extensive questionnaire surveys, and the very nature of the linguistic phrase "Africans in China" may cause confusion—it may mean Africans permanently living in China or those on frequent visits. In this chapter, we discuss these and other challenges for quantifying the African presence in China, and then propose some strategies to estimate the numbers for Africans in China in any one-year and that may be used to update quantitative measures that continuously monitor the African presence in Greater China. Beyond these issues of numbers, our discussion has implications for larger questions about the dichotomy between qualitative and quantitative methodologies in the humanities and social sciences.

With more than 50 journal articles published on the African presence in China, this area of study has now become an established subfield within the larger field of Africa-China relations studies. The migration and diasporization process associated with the African presence in China is fairly well known. We know that most Africans come to China as traders, though a sizeable number also come to study. These Africans are found in major cities in the mainland, Hong Kong, Macau, and Taiwan—what, taken together, we refer to as Greater China. Within mainland China, Africans are found in the main cities of Guangzhou, which has the largest and most vibrant presence; Yiwu; Shanghai; and, of course, Beijing, the capital of the country. We are also beginning to construct elaborate profiles of African lives and their interactions with ordinary Chinese and the Chinese state. A number of studies have painstakingly examined the African presence in these cities, documenting the opportunities found in their China sojourn as well as the problems they confront, such as run-ins with the police for allegedly entering, staying, and working illegally in China (Bodomo, 2012; Bodomo and Ma, 2012; Lin et al., 2015, 2014; Bodomo and Silva, 2012).

To date, it is difficult to know how many Africans are in China. Calculating accurate numbers about Africans in China has been an intractable problem. That problem is the subject matter of this chapter, not so much to provide accurate figures but to put related issues in perspective and suggest ways we can approach this research problem. Though calculating exact numbers for a large diaspora might be debated, having a more precise sense of how many and where dispersed is a useful undertaking. In subsequent sections of the chapter, we detail the problem, provide ways in which we have approached it, and propose ways to move forward. We end the chapter by going beyond issues of accounting to larger issues about research methods in the humanities and social sciences.

THE PROBLEM: ACCURATE STATISTICS IN CHINA?

One of the biggest research-related problems in China is obtaining statistics about foreigner residents and about entry-exit numbers at border checkpoints. First, China has no central unit for immigration, like many countries, whether at the Central Government level or at the Provincial Government level. In Guangzhou, Yiwu, Shanghai, or Beijing, one cannot just walk to a particular office and ask to be given official government figures about Africans in China. The nearest source for the official number of foreign residents is a *China Daily* report of September 16, 2013, that claims, "[T]here were 633,000 foreigners living in China by the end of 2012, up from 525,000 in 2010" with Beijing alone having 118,000 of these residents.[1] However, the same report is quick to clarify that "[o]f those who received the permits, more than half are family members who came for a reunion and the rest are mostly professionals, executives and professors, according to the ministry. Most are from the United States, Japan, Canada, Australia and Germany, and mainly live in big cities such as Beijing, Shanghai and Guangzhou." Excluded from the report are the vast numbers of small-scale African traders who ply their trade in Guangzhou; also excluded are most African students on government scholarships in China. To date, no government department or official has been able to pinpoint official numbers of African in China or those who enter and leave the country in any given year. Indeed, if one considers the vast number of foreigners, not just Africans, living in or frequently travelling to China with three to six months visa a year and constantly renewing them to stay in China, the figure of 633,000 foreigners is only the tip of the iceberg concerning foreigners in China. Such a figure is blatantly unreliable for any researcher in China who observes hundreds of foreigners staying for longer periods in many of China's urban centers.

The second biggest problem in accurately gauging the number of Africans in China is related to the research methods that many scholars have deployed to study the African presence in China. With the exception of Bodomo, Li et al. (2009), Bork et al. (2014), and Hall et al. (2014), many of the sociological, anthropological, and journalistic accounts have mostly pursued a so-called qualitative approach to the neglect and even disdain for quantitative approaches. Many scholarly studies adopted qualitative interview methods rather than quantitative questionnaire surveys. This is especially true for the journalistic accounts, where someone flies into Guangzhou for a few days with a microphone in hand, asks quick questions that require short answers, returns to their station, and the next day we read a sensational news headline, "Africans in China face racism!" Even the more sober participant-observation methods that require a longer stay and interaction with the research subjects shy away from interviewing large numbers of people. Some authors do not go into Guangzhou at all, for instance.[2] With little empirical base, these approaches can hardly address the issue of quantifying the number of Africans in China.

The third problem concerning the number of Africans in China boils down to an accurate semantic understanding of the phrase "Africans in China." Bodomo (2012) painstakingly analyzed all the elements in the phrase, including the exact definition of the term *African* (does it include only continental Africans or Africans in other diasporas?), the exact boundedness of *China* (does it include only the mainland or does it also include Hong Kong, Macau, and Taiwan?), and what does it really mean to be "in" China (does it include Africans of legal residence or Africans who regularly come and go or the undocumented?). It is clear that depending on how one interprets this linguistic phrase, there would be varying estimates in an attempt to quantity the African migration to China and the formation of diaspora communities there. In the absence of reliable government statistics, one possible solution towards quantifying the African presence is for researchers to make informed generalizations based on quantitative, empirical studies. In the next section, we show how an attempt of this was made over five years of research on Africans in China.

A QUANTITATIVE SURVEY

After five years of fieldwork in most of the major cities of China and in Hong Kong and Macau, and using a variety of approaches among 800 to 1,000 Africans in those cities, Bodomo and his research team painstakingly developed community profiles (e.g. age, gender, nationality) of those individuals. In this chapter, we discuss the challenges involved in quantifying the African presence in China before proposing some methods and strategies that we have used to estimate the numbers of Africans in China in any given year—which we estimate at half a million people—and that we use to monitor the African presence in Greater China. Beyond the issue of numbers, our discussion has implications for the larger questions about the dichotomy between qualitative and quantitative methodologies in the humanities and social sciences. The results are then summarized.

General Statistical Profiles of Africans in China

Collating the statistical profiles of the various cities visited in Greater China, we obtained 736 returned and valid responses, though our research team interacted with 800 to 1,000 Africans during this five years research project. In terms of gender distribution (see Figure 1), more than 80 percent of the Africans we surveyed in China were male. At the beginning of the African influx into China between 1997 and the turn of the millennium, African women were hardly among the merchant populations. A salient socio-cultural feature of the African family approach to business usually involves the husband who travels to look for new sources of supply for the business. With time, women began to travel as well. As African men became better acquainted with China, more and more women began to arrive and now, as shown below, almost 20 percent of the surveyed population included women, with some rather young women who are unmarried and yet to establish a family business. This number is destined to rise as more and more females come to do business and study in China.

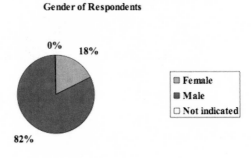

Figure 1: Gender of Respondents

Concerning levels of education, most of the respondents (683 out of 736, or 93 percent) have at least completed secondary education; among them, 288 have completed university/college, and 139 of them have completed postgraduate studies, as can be seen in Figure 2.

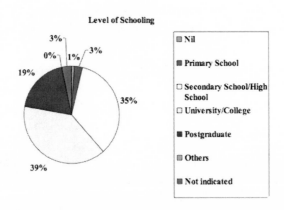

Figure 2: Level of Schooling

Most of the respondents (60 percent) choose to identify themselves as businesspersons or traders. Figure 3 shows that, in terms of occupation, there are more traders or businesspersons in China among the African migrants than any other profession, with more than 60 percent of them reporting their profession as such. The second largest group comprises of students at more than 20 percent.

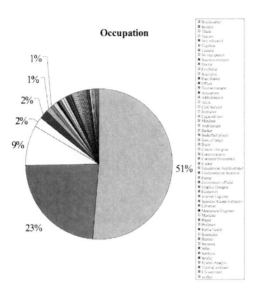

Figure 3: Occupation of the respondents

Most Africans in China are between the ages of 25 and 34, accounting for more than 60 percent of them, as shown in figure 4. These figures indicate this is a relatively young population in one of the most economically productive age brackets, which may vary from place to place but that is between the ages of 20 and 55, especially with regard to work involving physical strength.

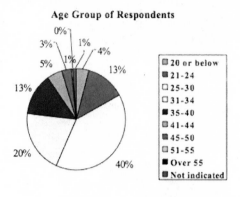

Figure 4: The Age group of the respondents

One of the most crucial questions we had to address frequently in the early phrase of our research was from which countries did these Africans originate. As can be seen in Figure 5, the top 10 countries of origins in our survey group were Nigeria with 125 respondents, Ghana with 87, Mali with 51, Guinea with 43, Senegal with 42, Tanzania with 36, Congo with 34, Kenya with 33, Cameroon with 21, and Niger with 20 respondents. This list suggests a preponderant West African presence in China, with Nigeria having the largest number by far.

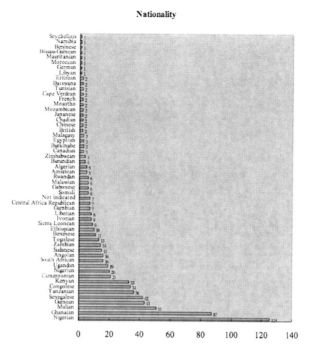

Figure 5: Nationality of the respondents

To date, these empirical and quantitative results detailed above remains one of the most comprehensive published on Africans in China. Based on this five year research involving qualitative methods (e.g. participant-observations at community meetings, market scenes, churches and mosques), and quantitative methods (e.g. questionnaire surveys, canvassing community leaders, gathering statistical sources such as the *Guangzhou Statistical Yearbook* that lists the number of Africans who stay overnight in hotels), we concluded there are some 400, 000 to 500,000 Africans present in China in any year.[3] This estimation includes at least 300,000 to 400,000 traders, 30,000 to 40,000 students, 4,000 to 5,000 professionals, 10,000 to 100,000 tourists, and 10,000 to 20,000 temporary business travelers. We do not claim to be statisticians, but we are quite confident our estimates are the most accurate to date. In fact, some Chinese government agencies have even started to quote our numbers even after they refused to assist us. We have never suggested these Africans live in China permanently; these Africans live in or frequently visit China. The phraseology "Africans in China" is semantically a complex notion; it should not be interpreted in the literal sense.

Reactions to Quantitative Estimations

Whereas some Chinese government bodies began to use our statistics, including the Guangzhou Municipal Academy of Social Sciences and the Yiwu Municipality, some scholars have questioned these statistics.[4] For instance, Castillo (2014), in his study of Africans in Guangzhou, wrote, "Over the last decade, Africans have been the most salient group of foreign residents and transient populations in the city. Interestingly, despite a lack of reliable data on the numbers, nationalities, and activities of these subjects, the hype about 'Africans in Guangzhou' has led several researchers to either lay claim to non-rigorous calculations or accidentally reify rumours resulting in figures ranging from 1500 to 20,000 to over 100,000 (cf. Bodomo 2010; Li, Ma, and Xue, 2009; Zhang, 2008). Unfortunately, these widely quoted figures are nothing more than speculation bolstered by media claims—ubiquitously reproduced—of an African population growing at a rate of 30 to 40 percent annually since 2003 (e.g. Branigan, 2010; Osnos, 2009). Over the last five years, scholars have attempted not only to determine the numbers but also the nationalities of Africans arriving in Guangzhou. This has proven all the more difficult by the highly erratic nature of obtaining Chinese entry visas, which seem dependent on the particular relationship China has with each African state. According to Bodomo (2010: 5), those Africans states from which the majority of Africans in Guangzhou originate are Nigeria and Ghana and, to a lesser extent, Mali and Guinea."

Some scholars have tried to make sense of quantifying the African presence in China, but others, such as Castillo (2014), offer only criticism rather than an alternative proposal for ascertaining the numbers of Africans in China. The latter approach does not study a community that the world knows very little about. In fact, what

Castillo (2014) and his related works rely on are dated estimates by some Chinese sources that claim no more than 600,000 foreign residents but deny the potential presence of some 500,000 Africans in China. However, as early as 2010, Chinese newsgroups, such as Xinhua News Agency, estimated the number of foreigners in China as follows: "China has become a major destination for international migration with an estimated 2.85 million of the 26.11 million foreigners entering China for employment [since] 2007."[5] Extrapolations or informed estimations are not new in statistical studies of populations and their activities. Scholars of Africa-China relations and other social scientists do so all the time: police statisticians estimate crowd numbers, organizers of demonstrations estimate participants and supporters, opinion polls estimate voter and other population numbers. Quantification and estimates serve the purpose of useful generalizations for policy makers and the public. For a transient and growing diaspora, such as Africans in China, this could not be truer.

DISCUSSION

Our discussion thus far has been concerned with only numbers. However, the issues raised have deeper implications for research methods in the humanities and social sciences. We believe that there has been too much of a dichotomy between the so-called qualitative and quantitative methods. In the twenty-first century, we think migration and diasporization forces us to use mixed methods to understand these complex human flows and exchanges. Pursuing an exclusively qualitative approach without a solid empirical base undermines our need to understand the numbers in and the dynamics of a diaspora community. The data from the five-year research project led by Bodomo (2012) involved qualitative and quantitative methods in order to generate reliable demographic and sociological profiles for African communities in China. Having quantitative *and* qualitative data is essential to the development of socio-cultural theories, such as the bridge theory espoused by Bodomo (2010, 2012), to explain the African presence in China.

It is clear that any deductions from quantitative data must be placed in context, in order to clarify the phrase "Africans in China" and to calculate their numerical presence accurately. To do both, our study used qualitative and quantitative approaches, often referred to as triangulation of method. Neuman (2003: 139) states, "[...] *triangulation of method* means mixing qualitative and quantitative styles of research and data. Most researchers develop an expertise in one style, but the methods or styles have different, complementary strengths. Since there is only partial overlap, a study using both is fuller or more comprehensive." In many cases, this strategy is applied to detect and correct the problems that occur when research is conducted using only one method. While we agree that the use of either of the two methods is beneficial in these cases, we believe that triangulation, involving the combination of these methods, is even more advantageous for research because it accounts for complex and interwoven phenomena. Another argument for combining approaches is that doing so facilitates the interdisciplinary study of Africans in China. Research on the African diaspora in China links several different academic areas such as African and Asian studies, linguistics, sociology, political sciences, and history. The combination of methods provides for greater depth and for us to examine as many issues as possible.

CONCLUSION

In this chapter, we have attempted to determine how many Africans lived in or visited China in any given year. We began by outlining some of the difficulties involved in getting reliable statistics about Africans in particular and foreigners in general in China. Official figures are mostly absent. Where they exist, they are not reliable. Whereas the Chinese government figures indicate there were only 633,000 foreigners resident in China in 2012, we believe the numbers may be anywhere around 30 million foreigners present in China in any year, given that the official Xinhua News Agency quoted 2007 figures to be 26 million foreigners in China. In the case of Africans, our estimates, based on five years of mixed methods research, tell us there were around 500,000 Africans present in Greater

China in 2012. This chapter proposes the future lies not in a strong dichotomy between qualitative and quantitative methods but in a skillful mingling of the two main approaches. As part of a future research agenda, academics and government officials need to collaborate more closely in addressing the issue of making available reliable statistics. Policy formulations in the field of Africa-China relations depend, in a significant way, on quantifying the African presence in China as well as the Chinese presence in Africa.

REFERENCES

Bertoncello, B. and Sylvie Bredeloup (2007) The emergence of new African "Trading posts" in Hong Kong and Guangzhou. *China Perspectives*, No.1, pp 94 -105.

Bodomo, A. (2007) An Emerging African-Chinese Community in Hong Kong: The Case of Tsim Sha Tsui's Chungking Mansions, In Kwesi Kwaa Prah (ed). *Afro-Chinese Relations: Past, Present and Future. Cape Town, South Africa.* The Center for Advanced Studies in African Societies, 367-389.

Bodomo, A. (2009) Africa-China relations: symmetry, soft power, and South Africa. The China Review: An Interdisciplinary Journal on Greater China, Vol. 9, No. 2 (Fall 2009), 169-178.

Bodomo, A. (2010) The African trading community in Guangzhou: an emerging bridge for Africa-China relations. China Quarterly. *Volume 203, pages 693– 707.*

Bodomo, A. (2012) *Africans in China: A Sociocultural Study and Its Implications for Africa-China Relations.* Amherst, New York: Cambria Press.

Bodomo, A. and Grace Ma (2012) We are what we eat: food in the process of community formation and identity shaping among African traders in Guangzhou and Yiwu. *African Diaspora* 5(1), 1-26.

Bodomo, A. and Roberval Silva (2012) Language matters: the role of linguistic identity in the establishment of the lusophone African community in Macau. *African Studies* 71(1), 71-90.

Bodomo, A. (2013) African diaspora remittances are better than foreign aid funds. *World economics* (Henley-on-Thames, England), 14(4), 21-28.

Bodomo, A. (2014) The African traveller and the Chinese customs official: ethnic minority profiling in border check points in Hong Kong and China? *Journal of African American Studies*, Online First, June 22, 2014.

Bork-Hüffer, Etzold, Gransow, Tomba, Sterly, Suda, Kraas & Flock (2014): Agency and the Making of Transient Urban Spaces: Examples of Migrants in the City in the Pearl River Delta, China and Dhaka, Bangladesh. In: Population, Space and Place (online first). DOI: 10.1002/psp.1890. *http://onlinelibrary.wiley.com/doi/10.1002/psp.1890/abstract*

Bredeloup, S. (2012) African trading posts in Guangzhou: emergent or recurrent commercial form? *African Diaspora* 5(1): 27–50.

Castillo, R. (2014) "Feeling at home in the "Chocolate City": an exploration of place-making practices and structures of belonging amongst Africans in Guangzhou." Inter-Asia Cultural Studies 15 (2): 1-23.

Cissé, D. (2013) South-South Migration and Sino-African Small Traders: A Comparative Study of Chinese in Senegal and Africans in China. *African Review of Economics and Finance* 5(1), 17-30.

Guangzhou Statistical Yearbook (2013) China Statistics Press

Hall, B., Chen, W., Latkin, C., Ling, L, Tucker, J. (2014) Africans in south China face social and health barriers. *The Lancet*, vol 283, Issue 9925, 1291—1292, 12th April 2014.

Han, H. (2013) Individual Grassroots Multilingualism in Africa Town in Guangzhou: The Role of States in Globalization. *International Multilingual Research Journal* 7(1), 83-97.

Haugen, H. Ø. (2011) Chinese exports to Africa: Competition, complementarity and cooperation between micro-level actors. In *Forum for Development Studies* 38(2), 157-176.

Haugen, H. Ø. (2012) Nigerians in China: A second state of immobility. *International Migration* 50(2), 65-80.

Haugen, H. Ø. (2013a) China's recruitment of African university students: policy efficacy and unintended outcomes. *Globalisation, Societies and Education* 11(3), 315-334.

Haugen, H. Ø. (2013b) African pentecostal migrants in China: Marginalization and the alternative geography of a mission theology. *African Studies Review*. 56(1), 81-102

Hevi, E. (1964) *An African student in China*. Pall Mall.

Kim B.-R. (2008) African presence in Korea. In Kiran Kamal Prasad and Jean-Pierre Angenot (ed). *TADIA: The African Diaspora in Asia, Explorations on a Less Known Fact*: Papers Presented at the First International Conference on the African Diaspora in Asia in Panaji, Goa, 435-444.

Lan, Shanshan (2014) State regulation of undocumented African migrants in China: A multi-scalar analysis. *Journal of Asian and African Studies* Vol. X 1-16.

Le Bail, H. (2009). Foreign Migrations to China's City-Markets: the case of African merchants. *Asie Visions* 19.

Li, Anshan (2005) African studies in China in the Twentieth Century: A Historiographical Survey. *African Studies Review* 48(1), 59-87.

Li, Zhigang, Laurence Ma and Desheng Xue (2009) An African enclave in China: The making of a new transnational urban space. *Eurasian Geography and Economics* 50(6), 699—719. *http://bellwether.metapress.com/content/h677on3h87w1l808/*

Li, Zhigang & Du, Feng (2012) "Kuaguo shangmou zhuyi" xia de chengshi xinshehui kongjian shengchan—yi xiang dui Guangzhou feirui jingjichu de shezheng. (Urban new social spatial production under 'transnational commerce and trade'). Chengshi guihua *Urban Plan*, 36(8), 25-31.

Li, Z.-G. & Du, F. (2013) Zhongguo da chengshi de weiguoren 'zhurui jingjiqu' yanjiu—dui Guangzhou 'Qiaokeli Cheng' de shizheng (A Study of Foreigners' 'ethnic economic zone' in Chinese big cities—A case study of Guangzhou 'Chocolate City'). *Renwen Dili* 27(6), 1-6.

Lin, L., Brown, K.B., Hall B.J., Yu. F. Yang, Wang, J., Schrock, J.M., Bodomo, A.B., Yang L., Yang, B., Nehl, E.J., Tucker, J.D., Wong, F.Y. (2015) Overcoming barriers to health-care access: A qualitative study among African migrants in Guangzhou, China. *Global Public Health*.

Lin, L, Brown, KB, Yu, F, Yang, J, Wang, J, Schrock, JM, Bodomo, AB, Yang, L, Yang, B, Nehl, EJ, Tucker, JD & Wong, FY (2014) Health Care Experiences and Perceived Barriers to Health Care Access: A Qualitative Study Among African Migrants in Guangzhou, Guangdong Province, China. *Journal of Immigrant and Minority Health*, vol 17, no. 5, pp. 1509-1517.

Liu, P. H. (2013) Petty annoyances? Revisiting John Emmanuel Hevi's An African Student in China after 50 years. *An International Journal.* 11(1), 131-145.

Lyons, M., Brown, A., and Zhigang, Li (2008) The 'third tier' of globalization: African traders in Guangzhou. *City*, 12(2), 196-206.

Lyons, M., Brown, A., and Zhigang, Li (2012) In the dragon's den: African traders in Guangzhou. *Journal of Ethnic and Migration Studies* 38(5), 869-888.

Lyons, M., Brown, A. and Zhigang Li (2013) The China-Africa Value Chain: Can Africa's Small-Scale Entrepreneurs Engage Successfully in Global Trade? *African Studies Review,* 56(3), 77-100.

Morais, I. (2009) "China wahala": The tribulations of Nigerian "Bushfallers" in a Chinese Territory. *Transtext(e)s Transcultures. Journal of Global Cultural Studies* 5. Retrieved 24 May 2010 from Transtext(e)s Transcultures database available from the Revues Website: *http://transtexts.revues.org/index281.html*

Neuman, W. L. (2003) Social Research Methods. Qualitative and Quantitative Approaches. Boston, Mass: Allyn and Bacon.

Müller, A. and Wehrhahn, R. (2013) Transnational business networks of African intermediaries in China: Practices of networking and the role of experiential knowledge. *DIE ERDE–Journal of the Geographical Society of Berlin*, 144(1), 82-97.

Pieke, F. N. (2012) Immigrant China. *Modern China* 38(1), 40-77.

CONCLUSION

ADAMS BODOMO

The various chapters in this book have demonstrated African diaspora communities in China act as vital economic, political, and cultural links—or bridges—between Africa and China, and many Africans in China are engaging in activities that form the building blocks of an emergent African cultural influence in China. This process of cultural influences among Chinese in Africa might also be the case, but this awaits closer investigation. It, nonetheless, is understood that if we are looking for ways to strengthen Africa-China cooperation, we must involve overseas Africans and overseas Chinese. While the first two decades of intensified cooperation (2000-2019) took its cue from a government-to-government approach, which was necessary to create a solid base, the third and subsequent decades should be dedicated to propagating a people-to-people approach to Africa-China cooperation. A people-to-people approach involves creating avenues for different groups of people from each side of the partnership—such as professional associations, academics, business groups, youth and student movements, artists, and sportsmen—to interact more often. Diaspora community members can play a vital role in facilitating contact between all these groups, since they are indeed already doing this on their own and possess the kind of "on-the-ground" experience that make them ideal facilitators.

Subsequent editions of the Forum on Africa-China Cooperation (FOCAC 2018 and FOCAC 2021) should dedicate whole working sessions to the role of the two overseas or diasporic communities—Africans in China, Chinese in Africa—addressing ways their formal participation can strengthen Africa-China cooperation, if they so wish. Therefore, we can enhance their participation in two ways. First, we need to streamline immigration rules on both sides of the partnership. There must be clearer paths to permanent residency and citizenship for Africans in China and Chinese in Africa. Police and other security forces on both sides of the partnership must respect the rights of diaspora members, including treating even those on the wrong side of the law, such as African visa holders who overstay in Guangzhou or Chinese illegal miners in Ghana, humanely. Secondly, we need to create structures and incentives to get diasporic Africans and diasporic Chinese keenly interested in strengthening Africa-China cooperation. Funds can be set aside for competitive bidding by various diaspora community groups to be used in promoting cultural activities that go towards enhancing the intermingling of Africans and Chinese. It is now time for governments on both sides of the partnerships to start promoting diaspora cultural festivals, diaspora business meetings, academic conferences on the African and Chinese diasporas, and diaspora sports festivals. There should also be reward and recognition systems to highlight excellence in service and leadership among diaspora community members on both sides of the partnership. This reward and recognition system should involve academia, wherein different groups of scholars interested in Africa-China relations could establish scholarships and award systems (e.g. best paper and book prizes) to recognize younger and established scholars who contribute to this area of research from various perspectives. Of course, more research still needs to be done by scholars on Africans in China. The research should go beyond the current concentration on the southern province of Guangdong, as the title of this book suggests, covering other parts of Greater China.

NOTES

AFRICAN DIASPORA IN CHINA

1. I would like to thank Adams Bodomo, Li Zhigang, Zhou Muhong, Xu Liang, Shen Xiaolei, You Guolong and Tian Xin for their help in my writing of this chapter. I use the term "diaspora" in the sense that Africans in China (or in any other country) is not only a migration group, but became a community with its own social network, cultural pattern and value system, which does not need assimilation (Bodomo, 2012). There are quite a few studies on the definition of African diaspora as a whole (Harris, 1993; Shepperson, 1993; Alpers, 1997, 2000; African Union, 2005; Davies, 2008; Zeleza, 2005, 2008). For Chinese literature referenced, an English title is used if one was originally provided. For Chinese names, the surname is placed first without a comma after.

2. It is reported that there is a boom of inter-marriage between Africans and Chinese in Guangzhou, China (Marsh, 2014).

3. In ancient China, the government had a specific administration unit in charge of writing authentic dynastic history. Therefore, twenty-four histories covered Chinese history from the earliest time to the Ming Dynasty (1368-1644). References of those dynastic histories are omitted owing to space limitation.

4. D. Ferand discussed the linkage between the giraffe and *qilin* (or *ki-lin*) in *Journal Asiatique* in 1918. Duyvendak suspected it was the giraffe "that caused the Chinese to sail to Africa" (Duyvendak, 1949). A story in Kenya offers a contemporary interpretation of the role played by this historical *qilin* (Li Xinfeng, 2013).

5. *Juyan Han Jian* comprises government archives discovered in Juyan, Northwestern China, "Han" indicates Han Dynasty, "Jian" means records kept (through sculpture) in wood or bamboo. Chinese scholars and Folke Bergmana, a Swedish scholar, discovered the *Juyan Hanjian*, which consists of 10,000 pieces dating from 102 BCE to 30 CE, in the 1930s. As official archives, *Juyan Hanjian* covers various subjects both collectively and individually, such as the political system, economic activities, military organizations, and the field of science and culture.

6. The identifiable surnames are listed here and involves people whose skin color is labeled as "black," such as Wang (1), Jia (7), Sima (8), Wang (9), He (10), Gongcheng (11), Gongcheng (14), Hao (15), Su (16), Du (17), Tang (19), Xie (22), Tang (24), Nie (25), Sun (35), Sun (40), Feng (41), Gongcheng (42), and Sun (55). The numbers that follow in brackets indicate the number of cases in Zhang's article.

7. Wilensky argued that "[t]he scarcity of references to *sengchi* and *zengqi* (here meaning *Sengzhi*) in nonfiction sources suggests that the Chinese did not necessarily link the word Kunlun to the Arabs' *sengchi* slaves during the Tang" (Wilensky, 2002: 8).

8. There are different translations of the title, such as "Records of the Taiping Era," "Extensive Gleanings of the Reign of Great Tranquility," and "Extensive Gleanings from the Reign of Great Peace." Yet the book is comprised of various aspects of literature from the Han Dynasty to the beginning of the Song Dynasty. A monumental work ordered by Emperor Taizhong (939-997 CE) and of 500 volumes. It was compiled in the Taiping Kaiyuan period (978 CE), and therefore I translate it as such.

9. Another case of his bias is the interpretation of *huanchang* (or *huanchang-wei*, change of bowels or stomach) as "cultural imperialism." In Zhu Yu's passage about the slaves, "They eat raw food. But once they are acquired as slaves, they are fed cooked food. They thereupon endure days of diarrhoea, which is referred to as 'converting the bowels (*huanchang*).'" This is in fact a long-time life experience in China as a vast land with its different climatic regions and food styles, which simply means it takes time for people to adjust to local food. For example, diarrhoea may occur in first few days when a Hunanese moves to Guangdong. Yet Wyatt translated it into "converting the bowels," and the word "convert" somewhat implies "being forced to change," which better fits the author's description of *huanchang* as "cultural imperialism" (Wyatt, 2010: 60). It is noticeable that Dikotter translated *huanchang* as "changing the bowls" (Dikotter 1992: 9).

10. It is not an "anonymous tale" as Wyatt claimed (Wyatt, 2010: 146). The story was written by a famous novelist Pei Xing in the Tang Dynasty,

published in his work titled *Chuanqi* (Legend), and was later included in *Taiping Guangji*.

11. Master Cui told his servant Mole the most salient secret in his mind (his love for a singing girl) and Mole helped him to overcome various difficulties to fulfil his wish. It is really incredible considering the master-servant relation. Because of the interesting figure of the Tang legend, Mole became a popular hero in fiction or drama afterwards.

12. Zhou Zikui, a Jinshi (a successful candidate in the highest imperial examinations) in the late Ming Dynasty even thought that *xiyang ren* (the Europeans) cannot be called *yi* (barbarians), but can only be termed *qin* (birds and beasts), because barbarians were still human beings, and Europeans were not human beings (Zhu Chunting, 2004).

13. It is believed that "India would experience many magnificent 'Transformations,' spurned and perpetuated by the race which gave India her first civilization and culture—the Black race." Wayne B. Chandler, "The Jewel in the Lotus: The Ethiopian Presence in the Indus Valley Civilization" (Rashidi, 1995: 105, 233-249)

14. This worry is by no means groundless. In a special issue of *African and Asian Studies*, although the editors seem to emphasize various aspects of African diaspora in Asia, most articles describe Asia-Africa historical relations as "master-slave relations." *African and Asian African Studies*, 5:3-4 (2006) (Jayasuriya and Pierre-Angenot, 2006).

15. Push factors refer to the condition of the country of origin and motive for migration (instability, poor economy, etc.) while pull factors refer to what attracts migrants (education, better social conditions, etc. (Bogue, 1959; Bagne, 1969).

16. A Ghanaian student talked about her experience in China, saying, "Others often ask me if I found Chinese to be racist, and whether their treatment of me as a spectacle – taking pictures, touching my hair, rubbing my skin, staring at me – does not indicate a racist attitude. I respond that I find them curious. Many of the experiences I had were borne of ignorance, not racism. Despite always being identified as 'black' and 'African,' I never felt discriminated against or antagonized, but rather treated with warmth and friendliness. Because I spoke Mandarin, I could often understand what people said about me, and they were rarely disparaging or maligning" (Baitie, 2013).

17. In 1996, the Chinese scholarships for Africans jumped from the previous year of 256 to 922 while the self-funded African students reached 118, the first time more than a hundred. During 1996-2011, there were 84,361

African students in China—36,918 enjoyed Chinese scholarship, while 47,443 were self-funded. In 2005, the self-funded Africans (1,390) for the first time surpassed the scholarship students (1,367). In 2011, the self-funded African students reached 14,428, more than doubling the 6,316 Africans on scholarship ((Li & Liu, 2012).

18. There are 47 articles by the entry of key words "African overseas students" (2003-2014) in Chinese Journals Network which contains journal articles and MA dissertations covering various subjects. It is impossible to discuss all of them. Reports and memoirs also provide information of the experiences of African students in China (Li & Li, 2006; Lokongo, 2012; Li, 2013; China Africa Project, 2013).

19. SASS was carried out in 2003 to evaluate gender difference (male vs. female) and cultural difference (Africa vs. West) in the perception of stress, with 200 forms sent out to foreign students at colleges in three cities in China, which contain 30 questions divided into four categories, e.g., interpersonal, individual, academic and environment. 156 valid forms returned with 82 of Africans (46 males, 36 females) and 74 westerners (32 males, 42 females). No group differences existed in the subtotal perception of the four stressors. Group variations existed only in their sub-divisional areas of stress. Cross-cultural orientation is suggested for foreign students (Hashim, et al, 2003).

20. It is an MA dissertation based on an investigation of 181 feedbacks out of 210 forms, a rather high ratio for an investigation. The author is an African student and the aim of the study is to get a real picture of cultural shock and adaptation of African students in China. It is found that all African students experienced cultural shock and the best remedy is to increase social contact with local people (Disima, 2004).

AFRICAN TRADERS IN YIWU

1. Interview by the author, June 2012.

2. Interview by the author, June 2012.

3. Interview by the author, June 2012.

4. Interview by the author, June 2012.

5. Interview by the author, June 2012.

6. Interview by the author, June 2012.

7. Interview by the author, June 2012.

8. Interview by the author, June 2012.

NETWORKS, SPHERES OF INFLUENCE AND THE MEDIATION OF OPPORTUNITY

1. Cf. Cissé (2013) distinguishes between "trade agents," (a category under which he assimilates our groups of coaxers, associates, employees, and apprentices), "entrepreneurs," and "temporarily traveling traders." Cissé does not consider "service providers." Cf. also Matthews and Yang (2012) who differentiate between "traders" and "consultants." At the same time, we depart from the wide-spread vocabulary of migration (e.g. Bredeloup 2013; Şaul and Pelican 2014), which in our mind does not adequately capture the potential of these actors not the status of their economic engagement.

2. In contrast to Meagher's focus on informal economic activity, we are not concerned with this aspect of our informants' networked practices and interactions as we are focusing mainly on established and typically regularized West African agents in China.

3. Interview AT n°31 on 13.7.2013 in Hong Kong; interview with the president of the African community in Hong Kong, LM n° 42 on 13.7.2013 in Hong Kong.

4. China Statistical Yearbook 2013, 12-2 Main Economic Indicators of Provincial Capitals, http://www.stats.gov.cn/tjsj/ndsj/2013/indexeh.htm (22 August 2014)

5. http://worldpopulationreview.com/world-cities/guangzhou-population/ (29 August 2014)

6. http://www.zeit.de/2011/24/Afrikaner-in-China (29 August 2014)

7. Meidah, or economic district n° 3 (Bertoncello, Bredeloup and Pliez 2009), is named after the first Arab restaurant in the area (Gaborit 2007).

It was Meidah's consolidated Arab presence (Bertoncello, Bredeloup and Pliez 2009: 106; Le Bail 2009: 9; Pliez 2010: 133; 137; Dittgen 2010) that to some extent facilitated the first African traders' inclusion in the city.

8. Interview LM n°14 on 16. and 17. 6.2013 in Yiwu.

9. By small-scale, we do not refer to these traders' retail mode in the markets of Ghana and Senegal. Rather, we distinguish between wholesalers and retailers whose capital stock suffices for sustainable business activities and those who render themselves to China with minimal assets and are thus extremely vulnerable to economic shocks (interview LM n°25 on 24.6.2013 in Guangzhou).

10. Interview LM n°24 on 23.6.2013 in Guangzhou.

11. Interview LM n°21 on 21.6.2013 in Guangzhou.

12. Interview AT n°21 on 28.6.2013 in Guangzhou.

13. Interview LM n° 19 on 19.6.2014 in Yiwu and n° 97 on 5.2.2014 in Dakar.

14. Interview LM n°19 on 19.6.2013 in Yiwu.

15. Interview AT n°15 on 22.6.2013 in Guangzhou.

16. Interview LM n°25 on 24.6.2013 in Guangzhou.

17. Interview AT n°17 on 25.6.2013 in Guangzhou.

AFRICAN UNIVERSITY STUDENTS IN CHINA'S HONG KONG

1. The author thanks Professor Moosung Lee for his advice on the research project on which this chapter is based. Credit also goes to Mr. Ewan Wright, who advised me on the language use in this paper, and to Dr. Mwaura, whose dissertation (Mwaura, 2008) has inspired the author to undertake this research.

2. As an update, the groups of African students and South American students still constitute less than one percent in the 2015 data, three years after the beginning of this research (The University of Hong Kong, 2015a).

3. RP010, interview dated May 26, 2013.

4. RP003, interview dated 22 May, 2013.

5. RP009, interview dated May 22, 2013.

6. RP002, interview dated May 22, 2013.

7. RP010, interview dated May 26, 2013.

8. RP004, interview dated May 16, 2013.

9. RP001, interview dated May 21, 2013.

10. RP004, interview dated May 16, 2013.

11. RP010, interview dated May 26, 2013.

12. RP007, interview dated May 24, 2013.

13. RP006, interview dated June 3, 2013.

14. RP001, interview dated May 21, 2013.

15. RP009, interview dated May 22, 2013.

16. RP009, interview dated May 22, 2013.

17. RP003, interview dated May 22, 2013.

18. RP009, interview dated May 22, 2013.

19. RP002, interview dated May, 22, 2013.

20. RP003, interview dated May 22, 2013.

21. RP004, interview dated May, 16, 2013.

22. RP006, interview dated June 3, 2013.

23. RP006, interview dated June 3, 2013.

24. RP004, interview dated May 16, 2013.

25. RP009, interview dated May 22, 2013.

26. RP009, interview dated May 22, 2013.

27. RP006, interview dated June 3, 2013.

28. RP003, interview dated May 22, 2013.

29. RP001, interview dated May 21, 2013.

30. RP009, interview dated May 22, 2013.

31. RP001, interview dated May 21, 2013.

32. RP006, interview dated June 3, 2013.

33. RP002, interview dated May 22, 2013; RP008, interview dated May 30, 2013.

34. RP001, interview dated May 21, 2013.

SOME EMPIRICAL AND METHODOLOGICAL PROBLEMS FOR CALIBRATING THE AFRICAN PRESENCE IN GREATER CHINA

1. More foreigners get China's residency permits. See *China Daily*, September 16, 2013, http://www.chinadaily.com.cn/bizchina/chinadata/2013-09/16/content_16972530.htm (accessed 10 November 2014).

2. The first author is aware of this since he is a constant reviewer of journal articles on Africans in China.

3. The latest figures for tourists staying overnight in Guangzhou hotels in 2012 was 542,500 from Africa. While these numbers may not mean 542,500 Africans visited Guangzhou since one person can come several times and stay in several hotels, when we compare these figures to those from other parts of the world we see how much more important those numbers mean for the African presence in China. Comparative figures for Europe (at 515,000) and North America (at 333,400) show that more Africans come to China than Americans or Europeans. In fact, apart from Asians (at 1,430,000) the next largest group are African occupants of these hotels. In all, more than 48,090,000 "tourists" occupied hotels in Guangzhou in 2012 (Guangzhou Statistical Yearbook, 2013: 508).

4. "非洲裔人员聚集事件调查：数万人非法居留广州 Fei zhou ren jing li jian xin chuang Guangdong" [Africans experience hardships in Guangdong], *Sina.com* (July 20, 2009), *http://news.sina.com.cn/c/sd/2009-07-20/095918257011.shtml* (accessed March 2, 2014).

5. Xinhua News Agency (2010).

CPSIA information can be obtained
at www.ICGtesting.com
Printed in the USA
FFOW03n2249010616
24626FF